T0065538

ANCESTRAL JOURNEYS:

A PERSONAL GEOGRAPHY

ROBERT H. STODDARD

authorHOUSE®

AuthorHouse™
1663 Liberty Drive
Bloomington, IN 47403
www.authorhouse.com
Phone: 1 (800) 839-8640

Published by AuthorHouse 09/08/2016

ISBN: 978-1-5246-1443-0 (sc)
ISBN: 978-1-5246-1442-3 (e)

Library of Congress Control Number: 2016909826

CONTENTS

FIGURES

EXPLANATORY PANELS

A NOTE ABOUT REFERENCES

This book is rather unique because many chapters depend heavily on the writings of my ancestors. Consequently, the core of those chapters consists of copies of the letters, journals, and diaries retained by my sisters and me. This means there is little need for referencing public documents.

When I do include information from newspapers and other publications, I note the source within the text. This explains why there are no footnotes or separate listing of references.

PREFACE

During the nineteenth century, individuals and families left their homes in eastern United States and migrated to Nebraska. The question is why? What were their motivations – expressed or unspoken – for journeying to unknown destinations?

This book attempts to answer those questions by examining the diaries and letters written by certain persons who traveled westward. More specifically, those people were my ancestors; but this book is not a genealogy of my family. Instead, my goal is to use the rich collection of diaries and journals written by several predecessors – and saved by subsequent generations – to utilize this unique opportunity for contributing to the body of migration studies.

I mined their personal materials to learn about their philosophies and political preferences within the context of local and world events of their times. Their migrations were influenced by the particular milieu in which they found themselves. It varied with economic, political, and social conditions of the period, which in turn, affected idiosyncratic lures such as land values and availability, discovery of gold, and job openings. The letters and diaries of my great grandparents are also valuable because they included comments about the turmoil in the United States prior to and during the Civil War and about interactions with Native Americans.

My eight great grandparents (see "Ancestors of Robert Stoddard") were all from families who were already established in the United States (i.e., none were born in European countries) and they were all born in the northeastern portion of the country (see "Birthplace of Great Grandparents").

Ancestors of Robert Hugh Stoddard

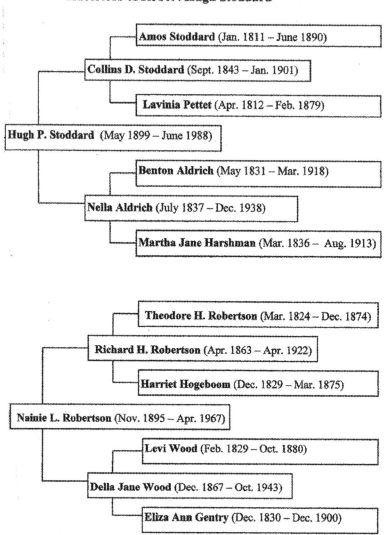

Amos Stoddard (Jan. 1811 – June 1890)

Collins D. Stoddard (Sept. 1843 – Jan. 1901)

Lavinia Pettet (Apr. 1812 – Feb. 1879)

Hugh P. Stoddard (May 1899 – June 1988)

Benton Aldrich (May 1831 – Mar. 1918)

Nella Aldrich (July 1837 – Dec. 1938)

Martha Jane Harshman (Mar. 1836 – Aug. 1913)

Theodore H. Robertson (Mar. 1824 – Dec. 1874)

Richard H. Robertson (Apr. 1863 – Apr. 1922)

Harriet Hogeboom (Dec. 1829 – Mar. 1875)

Nainie L. Robertson (Nov. 1895 – Apr. 1967)

Levi Wood (Feb. 1829 – Oct. 1880)

Della Jane Wood (Dec. 1867 – Oct. 1943)

Eliza Ann Gentry (Dec. 1830 – Dec. 1900)

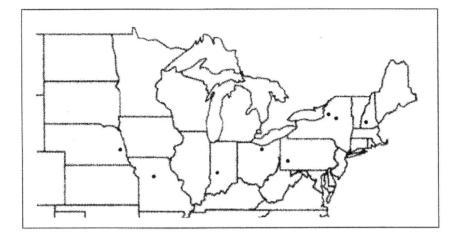

Of significance for this story is the fact that my great grandparents did not know each other, except for their spouses. Their individual decisions to leave their homes afford an exceptional dimension to studies of migration. A few of my great grandparents did not journey elsewhere and some did not keep journals or diaries (as far as I know). In most cases, however, their children who were my grandparents decided to live in eastern Nebraska. The overall effect was a process that formed the migratory history of my personal geography. The final chapter culminates at Sunny Slope Farm in Nemaha County, Nebraska, the place of my birth.

While putting this book together I faced several issues about what to include and what to omit.

One: A major judgment concerned a balance between two goals. On the one hand, I could include the entire body of a letter or diary entry along with a fairly rigid retention of the exact wording by each ancestor, even though some were quite mundane and only peripheral to the theme of this book. On the other hand, I could give my interpretation of their thoughts and activities. In general, I have chosen to glean what I believe were their intended messages rather than necessarily copying their entire writing verbatim. However, I did not hesitate to include the language that was common a century ago. It was fun, for instance, to read the words and expressions that my grandmother Nella wrote because I recognized linguistic characteristics which I grew up with. Also, even though I was uncomfortable with some discriminatory attitudes of the day (e.g., "the forests inhabited by savage men and beasts"), I decided to retain the language of that era because it reflects the assumptions and cultural milieu of my ancestors.

Two: My goal was to portray the life of each great grandparent and each grandparent so I organized chapters around a single individual (but I made an exception in the final chapter). I used wording that builds on previous chapters so, if a reader chooses to not read the chapters sequentially the relationships of families may be less clear. However, I often identified relatives and a reader can refer to the "Ancestors of Robert Stoddard". The effect of organizing chapters around one individual sometimes led to fragmented stories because lives were often intertwined. That is, I described some events in more than one chapter; for example, the journey of the Aldrich family to Nebraska is included in three chapters because Benton, Jennie, and Nella each recorded their own accounts to the trip.

Three: I also tried to balance a desire to authenticate or supplement facts while not making the end product a formal research manuscript filled with numerous footnotes and citations. I chose a compromise by including several explanatory panels, in which I added supplementary information that pertained to individual decisions.

Even though this book is my personal geography, my use of the personal pronoun is somewhat misleading in a two ways. One is because my wife Sally contributed to the preparation of this book in several ways: she helped collect documents that supplement information in the diaries and journals, she offered invaluable editorial suggestions to each of the versions of the text, and she devoted many hours to enhancing the quality of the accompanying pictures and the design of the book cover.

Another way my use of the person pronoun may lead to a misunderstanding is that one might conclude that it applies exclusively to me. In fact, all the ancestral relationships apply equally to my two sisters: Leora (Lee) and Evelyn (Evey). For example, when I wrote "my" grandmother did such-and-such, the statement could also be worded that "our" grandmother did such-and-such.

I think it is obvious that I am extremely thankful that many of my ancestors kept diaries and wrote letters, all of which were retained by family members. I believe this treasure trove demonstrates the importance of preserving written materials in suitable archival form until they are donated to public depositories.

In closing, I want to comment on two unexpected benefits I derived from this endeavor. One was the surprising discovery that several of my ancestors accepted and practiced matrimonial equality during times when males often dominated households. I have been truly rewarded that this rather unusual heritage of sharing work and decisions within the marriage persisted through the generations.

The second benefit was that I became quite knowledgeable about several of my great grandparents and grandparents, even though only my two grandmothers were living when I was born. From these materials, I learned more than just the genealogical facts of their lives – I was able to learn about their views of life and how they reacted to events of their times. Getting to know several of my ancestors has enriched my life.

Robert H. Stoddard

CHAPTER ONE

AMOS STODDARD

Amos Stoddard was one of my great grandfathers on the Stoddard side (see the family tree in the Preface). Although he never moved from his home place, his descendants were important to the story of ancestral journeys.

Amos was born in Lewis County, New York, and as an adult he remained on the land he acquired from his father, Richard Stoddard. Although several of his brothers left Lewis County and his own children later moved away from the community called Pinckney Corners, Amos apparently was an individual who had a strong attachment to a place and had a preference for stability and permanency.

The stability of Amos' residence, however, contrasts with that of his grandfather Samuel Stoddard, who made a major move in 1804. Samuel's birthplace was Spencer, Massachusetts, which was in the general vicinity of several generations of Stoddards.

I do not know the reason Samuel left New England, but he commenced the Stoddard movement westward in 1804 at age 54. Samuel, who drove a team of horses, and son, Richard, who drove a yoke of oxen, followed a trail of marked trees. They ended their journey in the Pinckney area of Lewis County, in north central New York State. Today the commemoration of these early Stoddard migrants stands as tombstones in the Pinckney Cemetery (Fig. 1).

Fig. 1 Pinckney Cemetery

Amos was a New Year's baby of 1811. At the age of 21 he married Lavinia Pettet. They had seven children (born between Nov. 1836 and Nov. 1852), three of whom migrated to Nebraska (see more below).

During most of his adult life, Amos farmed the home place. In later years, Amos (see Fig. 2) became more involved with "the mercantile business", as reported by the 1870 census, which lists him as both a farmer and general merchant.

Fig. 2 Amos Stoddard

Whenever he made a trip to Rome, NY, he brought extra supplies, which he shared with neighbors. In 1846 he built a small store (located across the road from his farm house and a short distance from Pinckney) where he could stock the goods and then sell them. Unfortunately that venture was more a service to the community than a successful business venture. According to the book *Copenhagen, New York: An American Bicentennial History*, published in 1976:

> Amos, who for thirty years added to his farming interests, provided local mercantile labor and supplied staples and groceries to the neighborhood, which was at the time when Montague and the south part of Pinckney were being settled. His generosity could not well refrain from granting time to those who were short of cash. He was very much imposed upon by those who obtained his sympathy and it was a frequent occurrence to hear that this or that customer had gone from the country in the night or on Sunday – they always forgot to settle their bills before going. Occasionally, fortune would favor a collection where efforts were made to defeat it, but in the main, business was more of an accommodation to the public than profit to himself.

After Lavinia died in early 1879, Amos remarried. He lived his retirement years in Copenhagen, New York (located a few miles from the defunct Pinkney Corners), and died at the age of 91.

As noted above, Amos did not migrate to Nebraska (or even to an intermediate location), but three of his children did and their lives relate to the history of the Stoddard migrants' decisions to move.

Curtis was the first male born to Amos and Lavinia. In contrast to his father, Curtis was always ready to try new adventures. At the age of 21 (i.e., 1862), he went to Wisconsin, where after two years he married Elizabeth Adams. By the 1870s they were in Gage County, Nebraska. However, nine years later when Elizabeth died, Curtis returned to Lewis County.

Although I do not have copies of any letters written by Curtis to his relatives in Lewis County, he evidently lured his sister Blanche and her husband to Nebraska. She had married Edmund Sheldon in May 1872 and by March 1973 their first child was born in Blue Springs, Gage County, Nebraska. During the next two years, two more children were born in Nebraska, but by the time the fourth child was born, the family was back in Lewis County, New York.

Collins, who was two years younger than Curtis, was the third member of Amos's and Lavinia's family who migrated from New York to Nebraska. However, he did not make just one move, as did his sister (Blanche), or even a double move, as did his brother (Curtis). Rather Collins wandered across the country in a series of moves that ultimately ended at Sunny Slope Farm in Nemaha County, Nebraska. The fascinating account of his various endeavors is the topic of Chapter 5.

CHAPTER TWO

LAVINIA PETTET

Lavinia Pettet, one of my great grandmothers, did not enter the migration stream to Nebraska. Nevertheless, it is noteworthy that her brother and some of her children did move to the state.

I do not have much information about her background or early life. The lack of data even extends to uncertainty about her name. That is, her given name was spelled as both "Lavina" and "Lavinia"; and her surname derives from "Pettet", Pettit", or several other variations. I have chosen to use the spelling she wrote (in her "hair" book).

Lavinia, born in 1812 and the second of fourteen children, married Amos Stoddard in January 1832. According to various censuses, she was a housewife all her life – as well as being mother to seven children (Fig. 3)

Fig. 3 Lavinia Pettet

A few clues to Lavinia's personal life can be deduced from the two hair books she maintained (see the Explanatory Panel "Hair Books"). Not only did she record dates of family members but the poems she composed and dedicated to many of them are a cherished link to my great grandmother.

Hair Books

It was common in nineteenth-century America for women to save a curl from their child's first haircut. This event took place when parents felt boys would begin to look different from girls and the occasion would preserve memories of a transitional period of babyhood. Also, locks of hair were sometimes taken at the time of death; and Lavinia saved locks at other ages (e.g., Amos Stoddard at age 40). Because hair does not decompose, albums of hair represented the permanency of family connections. Each lock saved by Lavinia is woven into a intricate wreath.

I believe this custom of saving a lock from a child's first haircut differs somewhat from the traditional practices in several cultures (e.g., some Native American tribes, Hindu ceremonies, and Jewish rituals) where the emphasis is on the cutting and removal of the hair itself.

Some of the braided locks (Fig. 4) are from the several pages of Lavinia's hair book. I selected the two to her parents, the two to her sons, and one for one sister.

Fig. 4 Pages from the hair book of Lavinia Stoddard

At the time of her father's death, Lavinia wrote:
> Joseph Pettet, born Nov. 12th 1785, married Nov. 5th, 1808, died
> July 3rd 1847.
> Lover of Peace thou hast gone to thy rest,
> Where the wicked will not disturb thy quiet breast.

When her mother Bethania Herriman Pettet died, Lavinia wrote:
> She was born Nov. 5th 1788, and was married Nov. 5th 1808. Died
> Aug. 15th 1860 age 72
> Again within those walls I see
> I see again that mothers look of love
> Glad sister tones in harmony are wove
> And as we used to sing at hush of day,
> The favorite simple lay.

In memory of her older son, Lavinia wrote:
> Curtis Rufus Stoddard
> Was born Sept. 18, 1841

Was married Sept. 2d, 1864
And died June 30, 1902

About her younger son, Lavinia wrote:
Collins was born Sept. 8th 1843
Was married July 7th 1864 and Oct. 6, 1887
And died January 13, 1901

In memory of her sister, Lavinia wrote:
Marritta Pettet, who was born Jan. 23d 1811, married Jan. 2nd
1832, and died June 12 1844.
Dear Sister, though we mourn for thee,
We know we should submissive be;
Affections tribute, we will pay,
Although thy Spirit, has soared away.
But soon Dear Sister, you & I,
Will tune our harps above the sky.

In addition to her three children who migrated to Nebraska (see Chapter 1), Lavinia's brother, David Fluno Pettet, also moved westward. He first went to Wisconsin, but later made a second move to Holt County, Nebraska. After farming several years, he moved to town to manage a store and manufacture brooms, which he crafted from corn that he and neighbors raised. Some of his descendants remained in Nebraska and maintained correspondence and occasional visits with the Stoddards of Nemaha County.

My summary of Lavinia's life is the following: All of her life, Lavinia remained with her husband on the land in Lewis County, New York State. Even though she was one of my great grandparents who did not journey westward, must have had thoughts and concerns about those family members who did travel to Nebraska.

CHAPTER THREE

BENTON ALDRICH

Benton Aldrich, the other (besides Amos Stoddard) great grandfather, was the grandfather of my father. He left a treasure trove of diaries and letters that expounded on his reasons for migrating westward, which ultimately ended in Nemaha County, Nebraska. Here is an account of this unusual individual, who expressed his justifications for his beliefs and ways of living. He was convinced he was right and he believed he had an obligation to demonstrate his superior knowledge to his fellow citizens.

Benton was from a well-established family, which had been in the New England area for many years. The "founder" of this Aldrich line in the United States was George Aldrich, who was born and married in Derbyshire, County Derby, England. The *George Aldrich Genealogy* states:

> George, brought up amid Puritan influences, had embraced with fervid and uncompromising conviction the Puritan faith of the founders of New England; and within a few years he joined the throng who left their beloved ancestral homes and braved the perils of the deep and endured the hardships of a wilderness infested with sometimes hostile people, to establish a nation in the New World.

Reportedly George declared: "God brought me to America from Derbyshire, England, the 6 of November in the year 1631."

Alfred Aldrich, who was the father of Benton and was among the fifth generation of descendants of George Aldrich, lived in Westmoreland, New Hampshire (Fig. 5).

Fig. 5 Alfred Aldrich, father of Benton Aldrich

He and his wife, Mary Farrar (Fig. 6) had seven children, including two who died in infancy.

Fig. 6 Mary (Farrar) Aldrich, mother of Benton Aldrich

Apparently Alfred carried on the traditions of his ancestors by being a respected member of the community and owning land (see Fig. 7).

Fig. 7 Notice of the Sale of the Alfred Aldrich farm, 1874

Alfred and Mary were grieved when the life of their older son (Hansen) was cut short when he was 14 years old. During his youthful attempt to play "lumberjack" on the stone roller he had been using on his father's field, Hansen was fatally injured when he fell beneath the heavy roller. Alfred was devastated by this misfortune and it seems he never fully accepted Benton as the only remaining male offspring. That strained relationship between father and son may have been one reason Benton decided to head westward; but it is obvious that another factor may have been more important.

From his many writings, both in the form of letters and his reminiscences in later life, it is obvious that Benton held firmly to a Jeffersonian belief in the value of farm life (see Explanatory Panel "Statements by Thomas Jefferson"). Throughout his life, he insisted that the salvation of the country was in the rural sector – not in what he considered the corrupting environment of cities.

Statements by Thomas Jefferson

Cultivators of the earth are the most valuable citizens. They are the most vigorous, the most independent, the most virtuous, and they are tied to their country and wedded to it liberty and interests by the most lasting bonds. As long, therefore, as they can find employment in this line, I would not convert them into mariners, artisans, or anything else.

~ ~

I view great cities as pestilential to the morals, the health, and the liberties of man.

~ ~

A city life offers you indeed more means of dissipating time, but more frequent, also, and more painful objects of vice and wretchedness.

His rejection of the values that his parents held was explained by John W. Irwin in his Master's thesis, "Benton Aldrich and the Clifton, Nebraska, Farmer's Library", a section of which follows:

> In later life Aldrich recalled that his formal education consisted of attendance at a common school for ten or eleven weeks in the winter, a summer term of 34 weeks at the academy high school at Saxton River, Vermont, when he was about 18 years old. He remembered he was a very poor student in grammar and language, but that he excelled in mathematics. For pleasure he studied

algebra and geometry on his own during evenings and Sundays. Later, he entered the academy; he was at the head of his class in geometry and trigonometry. During this time also, his father had bought him a surveyor's compass and chain. With only the aid of Davie's Surveying, he learned the necessary surveying procedures, and made plats for his neighbors.

It appears that his family, in the best New England tradition, was closely-knit, extremely individualistic, and. if not leaders of the area, was prominent. The Aldrich family in New England was a proud, self-conscious group, which prided itself on its ancestry.

At the age of about twenty, Aldrich remembered that he was offered a lowly position in a local bank because, he was later convinced, of "the good reputation of my parentage". Benton Aldrich, however, declined this offer, and shortly after he, like many other young New Englanders at this time, left New Hampshire forever for the alluring West.

When Benton wrote a journal many years later, he gave a similar account of the conflict between what his father envisioned for Benton's future and what Benton himself desired (which he described as follows):

> *My father earnestly desired me to take a college course leading to a profession, and offered me $2000.00 therefore in such sums and at such times as I might need. I did not accept. This caused trouble, though I did offer to him that I would take the college course provided I could thereafter, and at once, be a farmer. He declined this. I left home on borrowed money – from a schoolmate – which I repaid in six months.*

In the numerous letters (which were returned to Benton after his mother's death and thence saved by descendants) Benton wrote to his mother and sisters. He provided extensive information about his activities and thoughts over the next several decades. He wrote about his work and the nitty gritty of daily life. He told about his early work as a day laborer, his acquisition of land, his relations with his family and neighbors, his religious beliefs, his views of the Civil War, and his attitudes toward Native Americans and Afro-Americans. Sprinkled through his writings was the preachiness of this determined man.

Probably Benton's initial move from New Hampshire was to Eden, Wisconsin (located near the south end of Fond du Lac). He promptly earned money as a laborer in lumber camps and also as a hired hand on farms. However, his letters indicate that he soon began buying, selling, and trading farmland, especially after leaving the Fond du Lac area and arriving in St. Croix County, Wisconsin.

Shortly after arrival in that western Wisconsin county, Benton stated that "the prairies are beautiful beyond conception" and that he had "made a claim for 270 acres". To retain the claim, he had to make improvements, so immediately he began to build a house. To pay for the materials to build a house, he needed salaried jobs. He told his mother that "wages for farm work were $20 a month and $25 for cutting pine timber". The following fall Benton declared that he intended to bid on 160 acres that would be auctioned. His reported to his mother that his bid was accepted so he "must pay $7.00 semi-annually in advance". He described how 100 acres might be converted for crops. "The prairie is covered with grasses 3 feet high. Breaking can be hired at $3.00 per A. or $2.50 if you board" the workers. He continued by discussing how he might use the timbered portion of the land. "For the timber land I preempted, I must pay for it in one year or it will go to U.S. again. Fencing can be done with rails from my timber. I can split 100 per day. It takes 5,000 per mile. Slabs can be procured for $2.00 per 100."

In December 1853, Benton told his mother that he had "traded my 400 acres of school land for 40 acres joining mine. I had paid $50 on school land and got about $35 to boot in trade." In the same letter he reaffirmed his dedication to being a farmer. "I had an offer of being the acting clerk of the circuit court and also another clerkship, but I would rather be a farmer." In a letter to his sister, Benton commented that "Another chap and I are getting out timber for a grist mill. I live with a family by the name of Green. The old man is an abolitionist, a free-soiler, a water cure man, and a Baptist who now thinks the Bible a sham."

In his letter of May 9, 1854, Benton continued comments about his work. "I am at work on the river this winter, in a boat part of the time. Not as hard as on the logs all the time. Am getting highest wages, at least $2.00 per day." He also was concerned about his relations with his father. "Mother, what are Father's feelings toward me? Is his breast still full of revenge? I am aware he was very bitter one year ago." A third topic of that letter talked of marital considerations. "Oh, Mother, I want a home, and I think I know a woman who would make it look cheerful. I wish you were acquainted with her; I think you would be pleased with her." The woman Benton declared would make his home "cheerful" was Martha Jane Harshman.

Benton and Martha Jane (who was always known as Jennie) married the same month that Benton had revealed his intentions (see Fig. 8 and Fig. 9). A few days later Benton responded to what probably was an urging by his sisters to come back to New Hampshire.

Fig. 8 Benton Aldrich"   Fig. 9 Martha Jane (Harshman) Aldrich

He affirmed that "no one thinks more of his sisters than I and I would like to live near them". He then continued by explaining that

"I would much rather they would live here in the West. A man can live here with half the labor or make twice as much. Although raised in the N.E., I have always hated their stingy, mean ways."

In December 1854, Benton wrote what appears to be a more conciliatory letter to his father by mentioning these options: "If you want to buy property here, I will sell the two better '80s for $700 or offer land as security for $500 at reasonable interest rate. If you want lots in town, better let me buy them this winter." Unfortunately I have no information about the reaction of Benton's father to the opportunities in the West.

Probably the pressure to be a good provider increased when Benton and Jennie had three children (Karl, Nella, and Mary). During this period, Benton's letters were from Wiscoy. Apparently the family was pleased with their farm there, as evidenced by the many references to it during subsequent years.

It was at this time that Benton's letters were full of political comments about the events surrounding the Civil War period. On November 2nd 1856 Benton opined that "we are cursed with human slavery, and I am almost of the opinion that we had better separate and each take care of itself. I am not in favor of fighting for the freedom of the slaves, for I had enough of that to do at home to keep myself from being a slave."

Two weeks later Benton declared "My position now is, if we can't stop slavery any other way, we must fight."

The turmoil that affected the Aldrich family is evinced by the following two letters:

> *July 18, 1862. To Mother, from Waneka, Wis.*
> *I received your letter and the $150 draft yesterday. Sending for that is the only thing of importance I have done since our marriage without consulting my wife. Her father said if I was drafted he would get money on his coming crops, consisting of 50 acres of wheat, 25 of corn, and 25 of oats. My wife feels glad that I have $200*

in my hand. I took it from my pocket and was looking at it. Son Karl [who was 7 at that time] *said "What is that Father?" I answered "A draft." "Whose is it?" "Mine." "How much is it?" "$150." "Then you will have to ..."He could not finish the sentence. Last winter or spring he went to the Post Office, which is in the sitting room of a private home. While warming himself, two women kept staring at him. He did not know why. His mother* [Jennie] *asked what he was doing. "Nothing– only reading the conscription bill in the Tribune to see if Father was likely to be drafted."*

Sept. 1, 1862. To Mother, from Wiscoy.
You will excuse me if I write often of these troublesome times.
I find myself standing pretty much alone as usual on this war question. Of course I shall not fight for a slave holding government. You know this government are afraid of free speech and have tried to stop the tongues of those who do not agree with them. Now they have not yet stopped mine. I talk at every opportunity at home or in my own neighborhood. If they draft and I am drawn I do not know what will be the result; but most likely imprisonment at hard labor during the war. I am putting my house in order for the worse. My wife agrees with me perfectly. I have sold all of our cattle. I took them to Wisconsin where my father-in-law lives. After I had gone – the going was contrary to dictator Abe's say so – a lot of my townsmen and others got together and had a indignation meeting [sic] *and offered $50 for anyone to bring me back. Afterwards they offered the Sheriff the $50 if he would issue a writ for me, a bribe you see, but he would not agree to it. They made such a fuss my wife started after me. She got within 11 miles of me one night at 5 pm, nine miles of which she walked and carried Mary, three miles of it after dark.*

> *Three days after that, for I was not much frightened,*
> *we started for home in a wagon; we came home in 3*
> *days; and my wife has not been sick.*
>
> *The church folks here wish to get rid of me if they*
> *can. If they could have proved that I went off to get rid*
> *of the draft, they thought I would be pressed in the army*
> *and they hoped killed. Whether they will try to have me*
> *arrested for being disloyal, I do not know, but I think not,*
> *as in that case I should be locked up and not put in the*
> *army. By the way, they have been very still since I came*
> *back; that, of course, put a stop to the pressing business.*

The last portion of Benton's letter of September 1st relates to his and Jennie's associations with Native Americans. Their ability to communicate with the Sioux was achieved because of Jennie's experience as a teacher (see Chapter Four). The following is Benton's comments about encounters with Indians:

> *It seems that the Indians are killing off a good many*
> *of our Minnesota folk, report says eight or ten hundred.*
> *Some of my neighbors have mounted their horses and*
> *run to kill them.*
>
> *When we were coming home we met an Indian or rather*
> *one came where we were stopping in the woods to eat*
> *our dinner. As soon as Jennie saw him she stepped slowly*
> *toward him, and when near held out her hand and said in*
> *Sioux "You are a good man." After that you would have*
> *apprehended no danger, though he was armed to the teeth.*
> *He told her all about his tepee, his squaw, his papoose, two*
> *he said he had, and his game (whiskey). In short we – or*
> *rather they – had a good visit. At the conclusion he bowed*
> *himself out like a true gentleman that he was.*

I assume Benton's remark about the killing of Minnesota folk refers to the U.S.-Dakota War of 1862 (see Explanatory Panel "U.S.-Dakota War and Aftermath"). Given the clamor by the dominant power to dismiss the rights of Native Americans, Jennie's linguistic ability and rapport with this armed Sioux is certainly noteworthy.

U.S.-Dakota War and Aftermath

The Dakota (Sioux) people were aggrieved because of the repeated breaking of treaties (from 1805 to 1858) by the U.S. Government. For ceding their land, the Dakota were to be paid annuities to fund trade shops, purchase agricultural tools and supplies, and to pay off debts claimed by traders; but late payments by the U.S. Government caused great hardship. With no extension of credit and poor hunting, the Dakota became desperate.

Although many Dakota and "mixed-bloods" opposed any armed opposition to the aggression of Euro-Europeans, the more militant Native Americans persuaded Taoyateduta (Little Crow) to lead an army against the invaders of their land. After four Dakota (Sioux) men killed five Euro-Americans on Aug. 17, 1862, a major conflict soon developed. The "war" lasted almost six weeks with about 600 Euro-American soldiers and civilians killed. Approximately 1600 Dakota and "mixed bloods" surrendered and were put in a concentration camp at Fort Snelling during the winter of 1862-63. The engagement resulted in a cultural division between the Dakotas who opposed the armed conflict (with some even protecting Euro-Americans during the struggle) and those who insisted on keeping traditional ways.

This "war" not only divided Native American attitudes and actions but it also dominated the political climate of Euro-Americans in the mid Nineteenth Century. Benton's letters indicate that he and Jennie believed in tolerance and activities that might contribute to peace.

On the basis of Benton's writings, I am uncertain about his beliefs concerning slavery, the Civil War, and President Lincoln. Maybe the reason is not merely my interpretation of what he was trying to tell his mother but also his ambiguity about the right thing to do. Such quandaries were faced by most citizens in America during that period. Benton's deliberations became more urgent six years later when he believed he would soon be drafted. In the following letter to his mother on October 6, 1862 he continues the pros and cons of various actions:

> *Oct. 6, 1862. To Mother, from Wiscoy, Minn.*
>
> *I am sorry you are so much frightened. Your* [sic] *mistaken about my being a deserter. I intended to go to the place appointed, but I refuse to take the oath, which a soldier must take, because the Government were keeping 4,000,000 as good persons as I am in bondage. That is, I refuse to take the oath because I had conscientious scruples against it. Now, Mother, the day for shooting such men as I am is past. John Brown and his men were murdered for doing what the Golden Rules says we all must do. I am grieved that you should advise me to submit to do wrong, even to save my life. I have no right to kill an innocent man to save my life. Mother, your love for your child almost blinded you that time. But owing to the exertions of a class of good men, Mr. Lincoln has at last taken a good step and if drafted I will probably go into the army. Mother, if Lincoln declares the slave free on the first of Jan. I may then volunteer to help them.*
>
> *My wife and family are about to start for Wisconsin with bag and baggage. I purchased a small place about 2½ miles from her father's and have paid for it. If I go away, she wishes to be near her father. This explains why we will move. Our address will be Waneka, Dunn Co., Wisconsin.*

Two years later Benton and Jennie decided they should move to a warmer area where their fruit crops would do better. After venturing southward, Benton stopped in White Cloud, Kansas. There he wrote a very significant letter because he details the merits of migrating southward.

Oct. 1, 1864 To My Dear Wife

Tonight is Saturday night. Mr. Hawley and wife have gone to White Cloud village to a meeting and I am left alone–no not just alone for this low mud hole is full of women, dogs, hogs, cattle, mules, children, niggers, nigger children, and cat-fish. The women average pretty well, though two of them got into a spat today and called each other "Hore" [sic], *right in the street with a dozen men within hearing. I do not propose to find out whether they told the truth or not. The dogs are like dogs everywhere, a vile set. Hogs! Are a species which you never saw, having their ears near midway between the end of the nose and tail. They live entirely on the hunt-and-grab system and I think their meat has a bad affect* [sic] *on the people for Hawley's two nearest neighbors are in jail for stealing. The cattle are good but covered with burs. The mules are Mules! The children are what they are made to be–some well-dressed and intelligent, others Sand-Peelirish, others worse than that.* [N. B. Although the expression probably related to political events in Britain at that time, I do not know what meaning Benton intended to convey when describing the children.]

I will tell you how I came here after leaving you for this trip. My first stop was by railroad to Nevada, Story County, Iowa [north of Des Moines]. *From there two hundred and sixty miles I walked to this place. And, Dear, they were long, weary, dusty miles. But my eyes were open, my ears attentive and my tongue polite. I found no difficulty in getting any information the people were able to give. I hope my eleven-day-walk* [of about 250 miles] *will not have been thrown away. I hope to make you and our dear children happier and myself better thereby. Jennie, I could not give any idea of this country if I should try. It has great advantages and great disadvantages. I have kept the question, "Can we benefit ourselves by coming here?" continually in my mind. And I have come to this conclusion: that we can raise fruit here to our satisfaction, that we can grow wool cheaper here than there. Sheep are very healthy. The markets here for farm produce are very poor, corn is generally worth fifteen cents per bushel, winter wheat fifty, spring wheat thirty – these were the prices before the war. Farm crops are not certain as in Wisconsin, hence we could not think of raising grain for a living. Sorghum, sugar cane, grows so freely and well as to be a nuisance almost. The syrup is laid on every table as freely as water.*

Iowa is hopelessly cursed with "Speculators". I crossed the Missouri river a little below Omaha and came though Nebraska.

I am tired and cannot write any more tonight. You do not know how pleased I was to read that letter you sent to Hawley; they say I have been more cheerful since. Mr. Hawley and his wife are very kind to me. Good night. Kiss the children for me.

Oct. 2ⁿᵈ [Continuation of the previous day's letter]

I like the appearance of Nebraska very well. We cannot, perhaps, raise so good fruit as in Kansas but the land is cheaper, has fewer settlements, and in less subject to growth: the great evil here. We can get government land directly west of the northern counties of Missouri or west of the Southern counties of Iowa. In either of those tiers of counties they raise the finest fruit. The Osage Orange [maclura pomifera or hedge apple tree] *will make a fence, but it must be protected for a time. Fruit trees will require protection against the winds which are much stronger than in Wis. In fact,*

I have seen people who wish to leave solely on that account. Jenny, apple and other fruit trees do not grow here without care and attention. The caterpillar is here in untold millions, and the rabbits will eat the bark in winter if no preventive is used. An intelligent German in South Nebraska showed me his fruit garden which looked well. A part of the peach trees were killed down last winter and his southern cherries. Others did well. From what I can learn apple trees are never winter-killed in this vicinity. Farmers say, "If you can make your trees live the first summer there is no trouble afterwards." But deep plowing is not thought of, much less subsoiling. You see that I have no doubt about raising fruit, but we cannot live on that alone. What else can we do?

After sending the letter that explained his decision, Benton promptly left White Cloud and headed home to Waneka, then immediately began preparations for moving to Nebraska. When his daughter Nella told her experiences as a young girl (to her daughter-in-law Nainie years later; see Chapter 5), she reported that, after Benton returned home from his trip to Nebraska, he sold his corn, pulled down the shades of their house, spread the gold coins received from the sale on their table, and evaluated their finances. They then made plans for their winter-time move to Nemaha County, Nebraska. They designed and made special warm clothing for the girls and prepared for the first leg of their journey, which they started in February 1865.

First they traveled from Waneka down the Chippewa River and across Lake Pepin to their former neighborhood in Wiscoy, where they stayed several weeks with Benton's cousin, Levi Farrar. There Benton bought a linchpin wagon and a pair of large oxen. He covered the top of the wagon with wooden siding (rather than canvas) and built a wooden boot-box for storage of food and for sitting. Basic food was hard cakes made from graham flour, prepared by Levi's father (Noah Farrar).

Their route from Wiscoy was to Rushford (Minn.) and thence to these Iowa places: Burr Oak, New Hampton, Waverly, Janesville, Grundy County, Des Moines, Winterset, Greenfield, Red Oak, Fremont Co., Nishnabotna River, and Sidney. They crossed the Missouri River at Nebraska City and continued to the homes of two Hawley brothers (who, it should be noted, were not related to the Hawley in White Cloud). They arrived at the William Hawley home on April 11, 1865, after being on the road for six weeks. [N.B. Benton's connection with the Hawley family may have begun in Wisconsin and was renewed on this occasion in 1865. An earlier Hawley had moved to Nebraska in 1863, acquired land through the Homestead Act a few weeks after its effective date on January 1st 1863, and became the first settler in the Clifton area of Nemaha County.]

Mrs. Hawley was in bed with a six-day-old baby boy. The Aldrich family stayed with the Hawleys a few days while Jennie helped care for the new child. The travelers also received two news items; one was word that Benton's sister, Harriet, had died. The other item essentially ended Benton's involvement with the Civil War because it announced the surrender of Gen. Lee two days earlier.

The Aldrich family proceeded a mile southward to the 40 acres Benton had purchased for $50. They took the wagon off the running gears and commenced establishing a home. Benton and Jennie never moved again – they farmed the same land for the rest of their long lives (see more details in Chapters 4 and 6).

The motivations for leaving the East and then migrating to eastern Nebraska by this great grandparent are clearly revealed in this chapter. Even though this information meets my book's primary theme, I am including supplementary information about three organizations promoted by Benton because they further reveal the goals and beliefs of this great grandfather.

One: Benton founded the Clifton Library Association, based on the "social" libraries of the day. [N. B. During nineteenth century, these libraries were also called subscription libraries or membership libraries.] In contrast to libraries that were private or tax-supported, social libraries depended on the voluntary contributions of time and money by citizens of a community. Philosophically they followed the tradition of self-improvement and promoted a populism that encouraged individuals and small groups to foster the common good. The objectives matched Benton's views of life, so he started the first one in the State of Nebraska (according to a news item in the *Nemaha County Granger*, 1882).

In 1876 Benton convinced thirteen families to join the Clifton Farmers' Library Association by purchasing a share in, or subscribing to, the organization. The initial collection consisted of his personal books, which he valued so highly that he had brought them in their cramped wagon from Wisconsin. Furthermore, the association's library of books was housed in the small earthen home of the Aldrich family, along with the Clifton post office (established in 1868). By 1882, the circulation was 900 volumes per year and it had branch libraries in three other Nemaha County towns.

Two: Benton's emphasis on a community of self-cultured farmers logically led him to promote the improvement of farmers' lives through education. Thus, he enthusiastically helped organize the first farmers' institute in the State of Nebraska in February 1882. These institutes were two or three day meetings during which farmers and university professors would exchange ideas and information about farming practices. Benton's meticulous notes about planting conditions, cultivation, and yields often were the basis for a talk at several of the annual institutes. For many years in the late 19th century, these occasions, which usually included literary, musical, and social activities along with the agricultural talks, fulfilled an important neighborhood function. Eventually, with the development of state and federal experiment stations and extension services, the rationale for the farmers' institutes disappeared.

Three: Benton's humanitarian assistance to a persecuted minority was expressed soon after the Exodusters (see Explanatory Panel

"Exodusters") left The South, when the period of Reconstruction ended. Many of them fled to Kansas.

Exodusters

The Compromise of 1877 ended Reconstruction when federal troops withdrew from The South and the white-dominated state Democratic parties terrorized Afro-Americans. A major exodus of blacks, termed "Exodusters" (likened to the Jewish exodus from Egypt), began in March 1879 and continued for a couple years. An estimated 25,000 persecuted Americans migrated to Kansas, especially to Topeka where the Kansas Freedmen's Relief Association provided immediate shelter and assisted the immigrants in finding work.

Benton went to Topeka in 1880 to bring a few refugees to his farm. He probably was inspired by the pleas of a Quaker woman, who toured southeast Nebraska seeking help for those displaced people. He brought Louis Martin, Anthony Cloyd, and Almeda Green, who had an infant daughter. Benton gave them work and, until they could find other housing, a dugout for shelter. Although his action provoked local opposition, he was convinced he was right and did not give in to the hostility.

The three black workers moved to Brownville a few years later, where the men found jobs. Almeda, however, continued working for the Aldrich family for several years. Even after Almeda made her permanent home in Brownville, members of the Aldrich and Stoddard families continued social contacts throughout Almeda's long life.

In 1997 the Nebraska State Historical Society Public Archeology Dig excavated the site of the dugout where the refugees had lived on Benton's land. Interestingly, in the same publication that reported the dig (see citation of the Kennedy article below), a picture of the "dugout" residence of Benton and Jennie was shown (see Fig. 15 and additional references in later chapters to this dwelling). Although the Aldrichs' dwelling was more of an earth-house than a dugout and was more spacious than the one constructed for the refugees, it was an exceedingly humble abode (see Chap. 4).

This humanitarian endeavor by Benton is evaluated by Patrick Kennedy (in the Spring 2001 issue of *Nebraska History*):

> The migration of African-American farm laborers to the county was due primarily to the efforts of Benton Aldrich, a leading farmer of the Clifton community. Aldrich's attitudes are revealed in an undated letter: "They [the blacks] are an inferior race and must have friends among the more able of the whites or the low whites will run over them".
>
> Today these paternalistic views would be considered racist. In Aldrich's day, however, few whites, even those sympathetic to their plight, would have considered blacks intellectual or cultural equals. Although his views do not meet today's standards, they were above the cultural norm of his time and place.

Benton and Jennie enjoyed the satisfaction of fulfilling their dreams of being a successful farm couple – even though Benton's unwillingness to vacate their "dugout" dwelling peeved Jennie and may challenge the usual definition of "success". Even so, there is no question about their accomplishments, which were recognized in various publications. The section in *Andreas' History of the State of Nebraska*, 1882, about Benton Aldrich states:

> In 1869, 1870, and 1871, he planted an orchard of 1100 apple trees, now in full bearing, and in addition has 2000 trees two years old and 640 trees one year old, as thriving as trees are anywhere else in the United States, and his groves of fresh trees are an encouraging sight to the new-comer to Nebraska.

In addition to his apple production (Fig. 10), Benton supplied nursery plants to

WINTER APPLES !
Picking begins September 25.

50 Acre Orchard of Standard Varieties.
Wagon Trade a Specialty.
Good Measure and Load Promptly.

Orchard is four miles south of Brock and four miles northeast of Johnson, Nemaha County. Address,
ALDRICH ORCHARD, BROCK, NEB.
Cheaper than last year. No apples barrelled.

Fig. 10 Notice of Apples for Sale by Benton Aldrich

many places in the country. For example, many of the nursery trees distributed by J. Sterling Morton (the promoter of Arbor Day) were furnished by Benton.

Another tribute to Benton appeared in the publication *A Bibliographical and Genealogical History of Southeast Nebraska, Illustrated*, Vol.1, 1904:

> Mr. Aldrich was a strong abolitionist and since then a Republican. He served as postmaster for fourteen years, two years in Minnesota and twelve years at Clifton, but has otherwise been free from the cares of public office. He is too enthusiastic and devoted to his agricultural and horticultural duties to be concerned with other matters, and now in his old age his greatest joy is in the beauties and comforts of the home place which he has made by his past efforts.

Benton and Jennie celebrated their golden wedding anniversary in December 1904 (Fig. 11). After his wife's death in 1913, he lived another five years, but with the burden of dementia. He stayed with his son Alfred and daughter-inlaw Cremora on the home place until his death in 1918. He was buried in the Johnson Cemetery, the cemetery he helped organize in 1888.

Fig. 11 Benton and Martha Jane Aldrich at their 50th Wedding Anniversary

CHAPTER FOUR

MARTHA JANE HARSHMAN

One might assume that a woman who lived in nineteenth century America and who married a man as strong-minded as Benton Aldrich would not play a significant role in the overall migration of my ancestors. However, it is clear that Martha Jane Harshman was a woman who adhered clearly to her principles throughout her life. She partnered with Benton whenever they had to make major decisions.

Martha Jane Harshman, born the 1st of March 1836, was the sixth of fourteen children of John Harshman (1807-1885) and Hannah Smalley (1810-1883). Both parents were from families who had been in the United States for some time.

John and Hannah Harshman (Fig. 12), who belonged to the Pennsylvania Dutch community in Washington County, Penn., were married in Oct. 1827. Not much is known about their early years, but probably they lived the simple life of Quakers. For example, a family story says Hannah and other kinfolk sheared their sheep for wool, then carded it, spun it, dyed it, and wove it into a coverlet (a portion of which is in the collection of the Nebraska State Historical Society).

Fig. 12 John and Hannah Harshman, parents
of Martha Jane Harshman Aldrich

A couple of decades after their marriage, John and Hannah and their family migrated to Wisconsin. A partial description of their journey (which is from *The Harshman, Hashman, Hershman, Heshman family: a history and genealogy* written by C. C. Harshman in 1987, is the following:

> In 1847 the family moved to the vicinity of Garrettsville, Ohio. In 1851 they moved again, this time to Wisconsin. They floated down the Ohio River on a flatboat, then went up the Mississippi by steamboat and settled at Hudson, St. Croix Co., Wis.
>
> In 1855 John traded his first farm for one on Mud Creek near Waneka in Dunn Co., Wis. John owned and lived on this farm for about 30 years. In 1880 he had 400 acres.

Martha Jane, who was called "Jennie" (sometimes spelled "Jenny" by Benton), lived during the period when Civil War issues confronted most of my great grandparents. Her religious training emphasized the merits of peace; and after marriage she was influenced by the ambivalent opinions Benton had about fighting in the Civil War (see Chapter 3). Yet, four of her brothers served in the Union Army during the Civil War and one died in that conflict.

I gleaned glimpses of Jennie's life in Wisconsin before marriage from the prize-winning article written by Nainie (Mrs. Hugh) Stoddard) based on the memories of Jennie's daughter Nella. It appeared as "The Biography of a Builder of Nebraska" in the *Nebraska History Magazine*, Jan.-Mar., 1935. The section about Jennie's teaching school follows:

> Jennie's sister Margaret had been elected to teach a school term in Wisconsin, but when the time came she was unable to fulfill her contract because of sickness. Consequently she persuaded Jennie to substitute for her. Because Jennie's class included both Euro-Americans and Native Americans, this may have been the occasion when Jennie acquired some knowledge of the Dakota (Sioux) language (e.g., see the incident about her conversation with a Dakota man in Chap. 3). Jennie was such a successful teacher that the parents convinced her to finish the term, even after Margaret regained her health. In recognition of her work, Jennie was given a Teacher's Certificate.

After reading Nainie's article in the *Nebraska History Magazine*, Nella's sister-in-law, Martha Aldrich, related the following incident to Nainie :

> *When Jennie was only 16, she was helping a couple of homesteaders who had adjoining land and had built their houses just "across the dividing line" [probably a township or county boundary], with a covered connecting porch. One winter night a baby was due in each home. Although a blizzard was threatening, one of the men went on horseback to summon the doctor. The summoner returned home promptly, but the doctor was delayed because he had to assemble his medical*

items and hitch his team to his sleigh. Unfortunately the doctor soon decided he could not complete the trip because of the increasing severity of the storm so he abandoned the attempt to get to the expectant mothers. Meanwhile Jennie, going back and forth between the two mothers in labor, delivered both babies safely. A few days later, when the doctor came to those homes and found all was well, he said, "You don't need a doctor when Jennie Harshman is on the job."

In Nainie's article she reports that Benton liked to brag that his wife had helped with the births of a hundred babies, including several sets of twins. Probably Jennie's most difficult midwifery episode occurred at the birth of her own first child, even though she sought to minimize any difficulty by adhering to a rigid regimen of what she regarded as healthful living. She read the *Water Cure Journal* and similar works (see Explanatory Panel "Hydrotherapy"), believed in the benefits of good water, vegetarianism, and a limited use of drugs.

Hydrotherapy

Hydrotherapy, which was once called hydropathy in the English-speaking world, involved the use of water for pain relief and health benefits. It was revived from ancient civilizations by two British doctors in the eighteenth century, and then spread to United States, where, by 1850, it had become very popular. The *Water Cure Journal* soon became the primary monthly promoting hydrotherapy.

In her married life, she took a daily bath and about half the days she wore a "wet girdle" 8-10 hours per day. During her pregnancy she walked one to three miles and frequently swam in a creek. She was opposed to having a doctor at her delivery, especially one who might use drugs.

The difficulties Jennie encountered during labor were reported in detail (although I have partly rephrased portions) by Benton in letters to his mother, written Sept. 14 and Dec. 19, 1855:

Her pains commenced in the night, and the baby was partially born at 2 p.m. Her sufferings were not great, except for about one hour when she succeeded in partially expelling the child's body only. Here was a position in which ¼ of all the children in like circumstances die. Her pains stopped at this point, but the child's body began to turn black, and was finally as black as a stove pot. I immediately ordered cold wet cloths to be placed on her abdomen and limbs. This acted like an electric shock and her pains returned almost immediately and in less than five minutes the child was born – but to all appearances was dead. It did not show any signs of life for some time. Mrs. Allen said we had better cut the umbilical cord. I told her we had better not do it; she told Laura to get the scissors. I said firmly the cord must not be cut so long as the cord throbs. Mrs. Allen then said "I fear she will bleed to death."

You see, mother, that this was my first case, and if I lost the mother and child the neighbors would say I was the worst wretch on earth, besides being an infidel and working Sundays, to say nothing of some other peculiar traits, such as refusing to swallow pork, grease, tea, coffee, spices, salt, vinegar, and salivates – and also persisting in keeping a clean skin, breathing pure air and eating vegetable food. These are signs of a fool – but if I had lost my wife or child I should have been a wretch. So I thought if I was to have the credit I would have the management also. But to the case. I told Mrs. Allen the cord must not be cut till it had done pulsating and that the afterbirth must remain at least four hours before being pulled out.

We commenced to revive the child by putting a silk handkerchief over his mouth and nose and alternately blowing in his mouth and pressing on his chest to imitate breathing. After some five minutes he gasped very faintly and then remained some three minutes and then a stronger gasp and a shorter interval till in about one half of an hour he breathed regularly.

In the mean time I had his limbs rapped in cloths, wet in warm water and cold water, rubbed on his body. The little fellow lived and has not seen a sick day yet. About the time we got through with the child, the afterbirth came out without any foreign aid.

They all told my wife that the afterbirth must be taken away immediately or she would bleed to death and also that the child must be separated immediately or it would die. We thought they were mistaken. You have heard the result.

Jenny, by my taking hold of her hand, got up in less than an hour from the birth of the child, and sat in a common chair, and combed and braided her hair without any aid. I went to the spring and got two pails of water, put them into the washtub and Jenny got in and had a wash all over.

Laura staid the first night and helped take care of the child; since then my wife has done it herself alone.

When I first read those grim details, I was reminded how difficult childbirth was in the 19th century and how frequently mother and/ or child died. In this case, both Jennie and her child (Karl) survived.

Karl became, in many respects, a "chip off the old block". In his adult life he bought land, built a house across the road from Benton, farmed, and gave advice to the Aldrich-Stoddard families (an example of which was his admonition to my parents during their courtship, namely, that they should not marry).

In 1902 Benton wrote to his Farrar cousins, Sara and Lizzie (to whom he wrote frequently over the years after his mother's death) that

"Karl's health is very poor, we do not know how bad. Maybe he has cancer of the stomach. He suffers terribly at times." Although Karl died in August of 1913, his wife (widely known as "Aunt Martha") lived until only one month short of her 110th birthday.

The next child was Nella, who is the focus of Chapter 6.

Mary, the third child born in Wisconsin, left home when she was in her twenties. She and her younger sister Lina kept a millinery shop in Brock and then in nearby Julian until Lina married. In early 1895 Mary moved to California, where she engaged in both nursing and custom sewing until she married a doctor. However, within a year she died at the time of childbirth.

Jennie and Benton did not have more children until they were established in their new home in Nebraska. They must have been plenty busy preparing for their move from Wisconsin, making the journey, and building a new home. Although the migration route is briefly summarized in Chapter 3, a few additional details may convey the typical hardships endured by families – especially by the mothers – who traveled long distances by covered wagon.

In anticipation of encountering cold weather during February and March, Jennie and Benton equipped everyone with warm clothing, which required creating alternative forms of covering for the female members. After discovering pictures in a magazine of what some women in New York were wearing, Jennie and Benton designed and made a kind of snow pants. They obtained suitable fabric, rented a sewing machine, and tailored warm pants for the girls to wear during the journey.

En route Jennie must have coped with experiences similar to those of many other "pioneer" women who trekked across the Midwest. Years later daughter Nella recalled that they stayed a week in Grundy County, Iowa, because her mother was confined to her bed. On the other hand, Nella also remembered a pleasant night (which occurred later in their journey) when the family slept on blankets under large trees in a farmer's dooryard.

Upon arriving at their land in the Clifton area, Benton and Jennie immediately began constructing a shelter. Jennie, in addition to caring for the daily needs of the family, helped Benton construct an earthen house, a dwelling the Aldrich family always called "the dugout". She assisted Benton in laying slabs of local limestone to build the bottom portion of the dugout's sides. They constructed the upper portion of the sides and the roof with wood. The floor consisted of the natural packed clay. Undoubtedly Jennie was greatly relieved when the shelter was completed and she could devote her attention to a more normal routine of mothering and housekeeping. However, those duties were not her only activities.

Jennie carried water from a well located some distance away from their homestead, with the primary reason for the outlying location being that Benton insisted their home should be sited on top of a hill. They dug a well with a plentiful supply of water at a lower elevation, but that location required carrying all the household water on a regular and frequent basis. Like most farm women, Jennie tended livestock and helped in planting, tending, and harvesting the many fruits the family grew and sold.

The fourth child of Jennie and Benton was born in August 1867 after their move to the Clifton home. The baby was given the name of Hanson, the same as his uncle (who, as explained in Chapter 3, had not lived to maturity). Unfortunately, this Hanson also did not live long. A detailed description of efforts to save Hanson, given in the letter Benton wrote to his mother on May 10th, 1868, follows:

About two months ago Hanson commenced to have crying spells without, to us, any apparent cause. He would cry very hard at times, at others worry, but always very uneasy, restless and continually moving from one position to another. We tried to find the cause but failed and continuously failed till about two weeks ago. There were cases of Measles in the neighborhood; at one time when he became much worse we thought that that was the cause. From the beginning he had more or less fever, which wife subdued by usual cold applications to head, and perhaps to body, with warm bottles to feet and hands. Once in one of his convulsions we poured three pails of cold water in a continuous stream before he came out of it. He had his first convulsion April 30; they were about 24 hours apart at first, then oftener till Sunday evening when he had them one after another in rapid succession during nearly three hours. After this his strength failed. He had one early Monday morning, another about nine o'clock A.M. Then he slept quietly and sweatly [sic], gained strength and required but little care to keep his body warm, and his head was kept cool by only an often and wet cold cloth. We all had hopes for his life during this time. From Wednesday morning till Thursday afternoon his spasms were light and lighter [sic]. At sundown they ended.

To please the neighbors as well as for any possible good that his advice might do, we sent for a Doctor who saw him on Sunday morning before his worst convulsions. The Doctor told us what we well knew before, that he had taken cold just at the time of cutting teeth. He told us that what we had done thus far was right and that we must continue it faithfully for he could not live long without cold applications to his head and he warned us not to have too much hope in that. He said he [Hanson] had the worst looking mouth he had seen in 18 years of practice–there were seven or eight teeth nearly through, one a double one. He had more in sight. One of our neighbors, a Dentist, cut his [Hanson's] gums the Saturday after the convulsions started, which made him easier for a little time only. [Hanson died on May 7th at the age of 21 months.]

Benton did not finish that letter to his mother until after the burial event; the rest of his letter follows:

Our neighbors were very, very kind to us. Nine families offered any amount of assistance that was in their power – they could not have done better if they had been Brothers and Sisters to us.

Yesterday was a very beautiful day; nearly every person in the settlement was here to show us their sympathy. We asked Mr. Gilbert to conduct the services and to make a suitable address which he did; he invited all of those of our neighbors who speak in public, by name, to make a few remarks, two of them accepted, a general invitation was then given to anyone.

One of the neighbors, Mr. Reeder, made a Black Walnut coffin. He [Hanson] *rests now under a little maple tree about four rods from the house.*

Yours in sorrow, Benton Aldrich

Lina, the fifth child of Benton and Jennie (born in June 1869), was especially close to her older sister, Nella. Lina married a local fellow (Alford Butterfield); they farmed in the Clifton area and interacted with the Aldrich family in many social and business activities through the years.

Benton's and Jennie's sixth child (a girl) lived only from March to December of 1871. Benton scarcely mentioned her in his letters, but instead, he continued to lament the death of Hanson.

Before introducing the last child of Benton and Jennie, I am inserting an episode that demonstrates the enduring concern they had for others. This is conveyed through the following letter Benton wrote to his mother on July 6, 1872:

On the 8th of May the sailor, Mr. Hooper, was taken sick. Karl and I stayed with him three days and nights, then we brought him on a bed to our house where he remained 12 days longer. He thought he was able to go home, which he did. A few days afterwards he was worse and went to Brownville for medical aid. June 8 he had an apoplectic fit. I went and stayed with him till the end, June 15. I assisted in making necessary arrangements.

*At one o'clock Sun. morning I was at home and told the
terrible news to my family. Jenny mourned for him as for a
brother, my children for a teacher, example and friend. At
11 o'clock the remains came to our home. At 2 the funeral
service was held in our grove. He now sleeps besides our
son Hanson. He [Mr. Hooper] was so near and dear to us.*

The last child of Benton and Jennie was Alfred, who was born a
couple days before Christmas in 1879, remained on the family land,
and married Cremora Jackson Rawley on New Year's Day in 1900.
Her uncommon name warrants an explanation (see Explanatory Panel
"The Name "Cremora"), partly because it is another association the
Aldrich family had with the Civil War.

The Name "Cremora"

Lt. Robert Pinkney Rawley, a young commissioned
officer in the Confederate Army, was seriously wounded in a
Civil War battle. A woman (Cremora Jackson), who had lost
three sons in the war and lived near the battle field, walked
among the wounded to do what she could do for them. After
discovering Lt. Rawley, she realized she had known his family.
She then asked the Union officer in charge if she could take the
wounded man to her home to care for him. The officer agreed
because he expected the Confederate soldier to die.

After many months, Lt. Rawley was finally well enough
to travel. When he left, he said, "I have no way to repay you.
Everything my family had is gone. But if I ever have a daughter,
I'll name her after you." Indeed, when he had a daughter (born
Nov. 1877), he named her "Cremora Jackson" Rawley after the
woman who had nursed him back to health.

When Cremora was nineteen, she learned from her newly married
cousin Alice that Nebraska public schools offered one more year of
learning than at her home near Mt. Airy, North Carolina. Because

Cremora wanted more schooling that would qualify her to become a physician, she traveled with Alice and Elmer Jarvis to their farm near Brock, Nebraska. Upon completion of an additional year of schooling, she obtained a job as a "hired girl". Her work was to help in the home of Karl Aldrich, who was very ill and required constant attention from his wife Martha. In addition, Martha had the care of her infant daughter Elizabeth, her recently widowed sister Marcellus (Campbell) Ball, and Marcellus' three young boys.

While working for Karl and Martha, Cremora developed a friendship with Alfred and later became engaged to him (Figs. 13 and 14). Shortly before the planned marriage, she traveled to Mt. Airy to visit her family and to assemble, with the help of her mother and sisters, her trousseau.

Fig. 13 Alfred Aldrich   Fig. 14 Cremora (Rawley) Aldrich

When she returned, Cremora was met by Alfred in Auburn with a team and buggy. This seemingly trivial fact, however, uncovers the differing mindsets of Alfred and his father Benton, who discouraged the use of buggies because he regarded them as an unnecessary luxury. Alfred and Cremora were married in the Methodist minister's home, without family present, on the first day of the twentieth century.

Even though Benton indicated some skepticism about the eventual success of the marriage, he soon was satisfied with his son's success. Alfred, following the pattern of his older brother and father, farmed the same Aldrich lands. In fact, he built a house very close to his parents' "dug-out". On Jan. 4, 1903, Benton wrote: "Alfred has built him a cottage near our house, leaving Wife and I, for the first time, without one of our children with us."

Benton was elated also that this male Aldrich was married. This is apparent by what he wrote to his cousin Sara earlier in 1899: "It grieves me to think that only one life may be between the life of our name and extinction." I do not know how Jennie felt about perpetuating the Aldrich name; but Benton, who lived during the era when offspring carried their father's surname, grieved the rest of his life that his family name was terminated. This was because he himself was the father of only two living sons: Karl and Alfred. Karl and wife Martha had two children, one being a son who never married (and a daughter who took her husband's name). Alfred and Cremora had eight children: three died in infancy, two were daughters, and none of the three living sons had male offspring.

Jennie, who bore and nurtured their seven children, worked wonderfully and cooperatively with Benton throughout their married life. She assisted in their horticultural enterprise, and participated in their educational and social activities – and she tolerated most of Benton's stubborn decisions. However, I have the impression that two situations sorely tried her patience: the site and condition of their home. Carrying water uphill, to where Benton had insisted their homestead should be located, must have become an increasing irritant for Jennie in later years. The other situation that undoubtedly became irksome was living in the "dugout" long after they could afford a more comfortable home (Fig. 15). Eventually Benton relented and built a very nice house in 1911, but Jennie enjoyed that more comfortable home for only two years before her death.

Fig. 15 Benton and Martha Jane Aldrich with
family in front of "the dugout".

Summaries of Jennie's life and contributions to society are
furnished in three publications. One is the article, "The Biography of
a Builder of Nebraska: Martha Jane Harshman Aldrich" (mentioned
above):

> Mrs. Aldrich attended school meetings in Nebraska
> and had the rare privilege of being a woman voter
> because the Aldrich land was in her name. [N. B. I do
> not know the voting regulations for Nebraska in the
> latter part of the 19th century, but I assume she Jennie
> was an eligible voter because she held title to some of
> the Aldrich land.]
>
> In 1896 Mrs. Aldrich delivered an address, a duty of
> her office as Lady President [of the Farmers' Institute],
> a position to which she had been elected. She entered
> into the discussions which were such a helpful part
> of these meetings, offered prizes for best pieces of
> knitting and darning done; and met and associated with
> the outsiders who came as speakers at the institute.
> Among the latter were many professors from the State
> University of Nebraska. Some of these men became
> friends of the family, visiting at the Aldrich home.

J. R. Huffman, who was one of a group of hired men on the Aldrich farm about 1883, wrote later in the *Nebraska Farmer* of Mrs. Aldrich's influence: "One thousand farmers in southeastern Nebraska can testify to words of wisdom and encouragement from her lips in farmers' institutes. Her motherly advice, her helping hand in sickness, her soothing words to the dying, her sympathy for the poor, and respect for all the laws of nature, made her one of the sweetest and best-loved old ladies that has ever contributed to the greatness of Nebraska."

A second source is a news clipping (from an unidentified newspaper) written in 1911 at the time of her 75th birthday, which occurred shortly before her death in 1913.

On March 1st Mrs. Benton Aldrich was 75 years old. Fifty-seven friends came over to the Aldrich homestead with well filled baskets and gave a real surprise to her and Mr. Aldrich.

They have added many acres to the home farm and only a few years ago they built a beautiful cottage among the fine trees, which they planted with their own hands 46 years ago. It is a lovely spot surrounded by the oldest evergreens in the county [as well as one of the earliest ginkgo trees in Nebraska] and with great elms and maples for the background.

The third source is a short piece written by her grandson Hugh Stoddard (my father) written on the occasion of the first Pioneers' Memorial Day (Nebraska), which was published by the *Omaha World Herald*:

We met at the Benton Aldrich home under the gracious old elm tree whose spreading branches have encompassed so many gatherings. We missed seeing Grandma Aldrich – yet we were perhaps more aware of her than ever before, as friends recalled how she had cared for so many through the critical hours when life hung in the balance, of mothers she helped as they brought new life into the world, of children who received their entire school at "Grandma's" house.

CHAPTER FIVE

COLLINS D. STODDARD

Collins DeWayne Stoddard, my paternal grandfather, was a member of the second generation of ancestors I researched for the purpose of understanding motives for moving to Nebraska. Collins undertook a series of moves from north central New York State before he eventually settled at Sunny Slope Farm in Nemaha County. His movements involved many changes in jobs and locations; and he did not leave written materials during several periods in his life.

Nevertheless, a diary for one year, letters to his fiancé, and miscellaneous documents provide hints about his reasons various moves.

Collins (who often identified himself as "C.D."), was the second son of Amos and Lavinia Stoddard; he was born on the 9th of September 1843. Not only were he and older brother Curtis (Fig. 17) good friends throughout their lives but apparently the two of them influenced the migration of other members of the family.

When Collins was a teenager he did some farming and worked as an apprentice painter for his brother-in-law. At age 21 Collins married Eliza Leonard, and a year later they had a boy who died in infancy.

Fig. 16 Collins and Curtis Stoddard

Although the tragedy of the infant's death and the break-up of the marriage may have triggered Collins' desire to leave the region, it appears he had a peripatetic yearning for change. For the next twenty years he did a variety of jobs in numerous places. Although there are several gaps in information about his whereabouts prior to arriving in Nebraska, some locations can be deduced from teaching certificates. They indicate that he was in both Yorktown, Delaware County, Indiana and in DeWitt County, Illinois, during 1866. His location is not documented for the next two years, but he was in Nodaway Co., Missouri, by 1870.

Collins kept a diary for the year 1870, but information about his thoughts and activities were limited. This is partly because the diary booklet provided only a few lines and partly because he usually used some of the precious space to comment on the weather. Other limitations to gaining information from his diary were his use of incomplete sentences, minimal punctuation, and numerous misspelled words (even though on June 4th he prided himself in winning a spelling contest). Consequently, I chose to include only a few days of the year. The following entries are a mixture of his wording and my interpretation of what I believe intended to say follows:

> *Sat. 1 January 1870. At B's before starting for home with 2 boots & 3 coats on. Stop at Highlocks for dinner & where I left my horses. I went on foot to Maryville where I stayed with Norricks over night*

> *Sun. 9 Jan. Singing at the school house.*

This reference to singing takes on special meaning in Collins' life. He bought song books and copied the lyrics of tunes. And he frequently participated in singing events at schools, other public places, and in homes. His eagerness to sing led to a significant event later in his life (which appears later in this chapter). Sections from the rest of his 1870 diary follow:

> *Feb. 2 Went with Alpha Heflin to a debate; the topic was "Horses vs. Steam Power".*

> *Fri. 4 Feb. David Cicero & I went to a spelling school, where I spelled them all down.*

> *Fri. 25 Feb. We held closing exercises, which completes my three months at Pleasant Hill School.*

> *Mon. 28 Feb. I weigh 180 lbs. I went to Mr. Toel's house to begin painting his house for 16/- per day plus board and washing.*

> *Tues. 1 Mar. I got a horse from Mel Heflin & went to town where I got brushes. Then I went to Shanks for dinner. I stayed at Woodards over night.*

> *Thurs. 17 Mar. Today I helped fix a calf pen, dig a cellar, and paint some closets.*

Sun. 10 Apr. I went to sing at Pleasant Hill School, then I went to Mr. Swallows for dinner, then back to Mr. Scudders for the night.

Sat. 30 Apr. I went to see Mr. Griffiths, where I bought a pony saddle for $87.00.

Fri. 9 Dec. I had a full school of pupils; we studied spelling & declamations. Later I went across the river to church at Maryville. I stopped at Shanks and then went home with Mr. Frazee.

Wed. 21 Dec. Thirteen scholars today. After school I went to get my pony and then go to Mr. McKees to stay overnight and get one month's wages.

Thurs. 29 Dec. 1870 I attended The Teachers Institute at Maryville.

In the early 1870s, Collins moved to Gage County, Nebraska, probably because his brother (Curtis) and sister (Blanche) were living there. During the next few years Collins was a second grade teacher in various county schools in Gage County and later in Nemaha County. [N. B. The school "years" were rarely more than a few months during the dormant agricultural season. As an example, in 1876 he taught for only 60 days–for which he earned $90.]

In October of 1871 Collins married Catherine (Kitty) Dunn in Iowa (with one witness being his brother Curtis). A month later he acquired lots in Blue Springs, Nebraska, but by February 1879 the family moved to DeWitt, Nebraska. During the next few years Collins bought and farmed land in the area; and the couple became parents to three children (born 1873, 1876, and 1879). Collins' life changed abruptly in early 1887 when Kitty died.

In July 1887 Collins traded his farm for part ownership in a store in DeWitt. He made this change because it would be possible for him to be close to his children since there were living quarters on the second floor of the store. That living arrangement was sufficient for his family's basic requirements; but Collins felt his children needed a mother. This was a primary motive for his venturing to send a letter to Nella Aldrich in July 1887.

It may be that Collins thought about several women who would consider marriage; but the person who is relevant for this story was Nella Aldrich. He may have met her at a singing school several years earlier because Jennie Aldrich and her daughters often attended such. In any case, he undoubtedly already knew her when he went to get his mail at the Clifton Post Office, which was located in the Aldrich home. While there, Collins would often stay to sing with the Aldrich daughters. Those happy memories probably served as sufficient incentive for Collins to compose the following letter:

June 28 '87   DeWitt, Neb. Miss Nellie [sic] *Aldrich.*

Dear Friend.

Pardon the liberty I have taken in addressing you. Loneliness & want of companionship is my excuse. I must be brief & explain. On the 28th of Jan. last after a long & painful illness, my wife & companion bid farewell to earth & its sorrows for a home beyond the skies & I was left with 3 children. Mattie now 14, Francis 11 & Tom 8 years old. What to do I know not & hardly know what I have done except that I have kept the family together; tho girl has done her best she could, but she is too young to manage & after studying the matter over I decided to write you, knowing no other to whom I could give the place. nor do I know whether you are single or not. Will you please kindly to answer this & if you are not free to open correspondence with me or for any other reason object to doing so then destroy this, but let me hear from you.

> *With kind regards to your father & mother. I remain yours in friendship,*
>
> *C. D. Stoddard*

Nella's reply was positive (see Chap. 6), so Collins pursued what he hoped would lead to marriage. In answer to Nella's query about his current situation, Collins wrote one letter that briefly described his work (see July 6 below), but he evidently wanted to talk more directly; and by the end of July he traveled to the Aldrich home to visit Nella (see his letter of July 26th). Subsequent correspondence indicates that during their short time together they agreed to a fairly firm commitment.

Collins and Nella soon became more acquainted through their many frequent letters. Both of them often included comments about other members of their families: Nella mentioned her younger sister Lina and Collins reported on both Lina and his daughter Mattie. The correspondence, which expanded on these observations, follows:

> *July 6, 1887. I traded my farm for a store and stock of general merchandise. During the 15 months since then, I have built up a very good trade considering the amount I invested. I always wanted to be a merchant ever since I left home. My Father began in the mercantile business when I was 3 years old and I was brought up at the same.*
>
> *Just as soon as I could raise enough to start a business, I did so. We live upstairs over the store. I have 4 rooms.*
>
> *July 26, 1887 I reached home safely last eve by 5:30; I found all well. Tom met me at the train. He was glad to see papa again. I have talked with my aunt & daughter & they are both pleased at the prospect of marriage & they did not care how soon. Aunt says the house needs a head. Mattie is stout enough & has time enough to do all the work if only someone could tell or show how.*

School begins the first of Sept. so I think we had best make that the time for our wedding.

July 30, 1887. Mattie goes with me to sing in church. Francis is tinkering with tools & wants to be a carpenter. He has made himself a work bench & shop in the barn & prefers working there rather than playing. But <u>Tom</u>, I can't contrive what to do with him. He's too young to do much and I have little for him to do.

You asked how I spent Sundays after church hours. Sometimes I go to sleep, sometimes take a walk & again, sometimes spend the day with friends. To hire a team to go to the country costs too much to be indulged in often. I frequently read until tired.

Aug. 11, 1887. My partner has proposed to draw out his share. I was in hopes he had become better satisfied but it seems not. He wants a bid; I think I will offer my note for one year whether he accepts or not. When he quits I will need you the more.

Aug. 12, 1887. Well, a little about Lina. I found her a place to work & she went Wed. eve. Yester eve she came back & had a good cry. She was homesick & disgruntled with the scandal she heard. I laughed at her about her first experience as a hired girl & about being homesick. If there is anything I despise in man or woman, it is going about with all the news on their tongues. It seems a woman (I can not call her a lady) came to the place Lina was & two women let their tongues loose. I do not wonder she did not feel at home for I know she is not used to such talk at home.

She thought, if she could stay here with us, she would not be homesick any more. Now do not think that Lina is an expense or care upon me for she is not. I may not be able to pay wages for her work, but have plenty that needs doing to more than pay board for some time & if she wants to try some other place to work after a while she can do so.

Aug. 15, 1887. Tis Sabbath PM. I went to church this morning, but I came home sick with cramps colic Not knowing what else to do, I went to the drug store & got a dose of brandy & cinnamon, which eased my pain but made me a little dizzy. I feel better now.

You asked in your letter if I kept [the store] *open Sunday. No surely not* [intentionally], *but living over the store means that many times I am seriously annoyed by persons wanting to get something they forgot on Saturday. Sometimes I open the back door & sometimes not. I'd rather not be near the store at all on Sunday. But I can not always be away.*

Sep. 1, 1887. I gave notice in the paper last week that I would not trust anyone. It will be hard to refuse some & will doubtless offend some, but I had rather lose the customer than to lose bad accounts. And I intend to be firm & deny all alike & make cash an object by reducing prices.

Sep. 13, 1887. I went to church alone in the morning & after dinner I went to visit with Kittie's family. I had thought if all was well to ask as many of Kittie's folks as cared to call upon us on Sunday the 9th. What do you think of it? I thought it might be well to have an infair dinner, not necessarily anything very extra, but a good social time. [N.B. An infair was a party given by newlyweds, especially by a husband welcoming the bride to his home.]

Sep. 21, 1887. I am a little embarrassed in business on account of buying Mr. M. out. I hope soon to have all straight again, but now I have to hire some money for a time & reduce my stock, I bought more on the strength of Mr. M.'s capital than I can carry alone. But am glad he is gone (moved away yesterday).

In answer to your question about whether there would be adequate lodging for your family if they came to DeWitt for a infair, I can assure you that we have had sufficient space on earlier occasions. When I was married before, we had about 20 at the house & we accommodated everyone. At another time we were caught away from home in a rain & detained by high water. That night 16 men, women & children slept in one bed on the floor. We slept this way, with the long marks showing the males and the short ones the females: |"||"||"||"|. You see I am used to being crowded & dont mind it & as many as you choose to invite will be welcome.

Oct. 2, 1887. Have a new front onto the store making it much lighter and pleasanter. I was wondering if the noise on the street would keep you awake. My bed is right at the front over the walk & there are persons on the street until midnight every night & then some early birds about 5 in the morning, besides the watch who is up all night.

A few days later Collins traveled to the Aldrich home where he and Nella were married, then the couple returned to DeWitt for an infair and commenced living in the apartment above his store.

There is very little information about Collins after he quit writing letters to his fiancé. I have assumed that the picture of Collins (Fig. 17) was taken about this time.

Fig.17 Collins D. Stoddard, 1887

Much of Collins' life centered on his mercantile business (Fig. 18). Other peeks into Collins' life can be obtained from advertisements and notices in the *DeWitt Times.*

Fig.18 Keys to Collins Stoddard's Store

In the fall of 1887 Collins ran an ad in the newspaper that related to the largest earthquake in Nebraska up to that time (see Explanatory Panel "Ad in DeWitt Timex, #1"). In October, the newspaper reported that "C.D. has greatly improved the appearance of his store by changing the front."

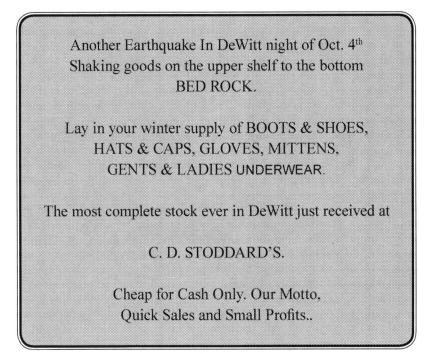

Another Earthquake In DeWitt night of Oct. 4th
Shaking goods on the upper shelf to the bottom
BED ROCK.

Lay in your winter supply of BOOTS & SHOES,
HATS & CAPS, GLOVES, MITTENS,
GENTS & LADIES UNDERWEAR.

The most complete stock ever in DeWitt just received at

C. D. STODDARD'S.

Cheap for Cash Only. Our Motto,
Quick Sales and Small Profits..

Two months later the *DeWitt Times* informed readers that "C. D. Stoddard has a fine wolf robe, that he is giving away with a fine quality of cigars. Buy 25 cents worth of cigars and get a ticket on the robe." A typical ad urging buyers to take advantage of bargains on clothing, groceries, and garden supplies (see Explanatory Panel "Ad in DeWitt Times, #2") was the following, which appeared in April 1888.

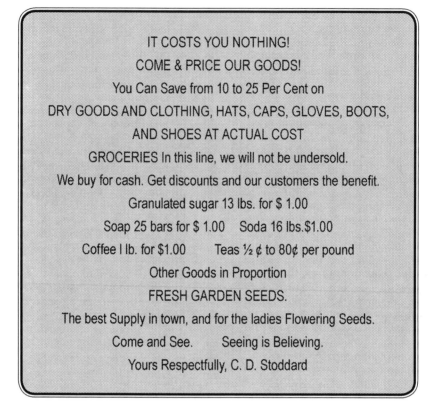

IT COSTS YOU NOTHING!

COME & PRICE OUR GOODS!

You Can Save from 10 to 25 Per Cent on

DRY GOODS AND CLOTHING, HATS, CAPS, GLOVES, BOOTS,

AND SHOES AT ACTUAL COST

GROCERIES In this line, we will not be undersold.

We buy for cash. Get discounts and our customers the benefit.

Granulated sugar 13 lbs. for $ 1.00

Soap 25 bars for $ 1.00   Soda 16 lbs.$1.00

Coffee I lb. for $1.00   Teas ½ ¢ to 80¢ per pound

Other Goods in Proportion

FRESH GARDEN SEEDS.

The best Supply in town, and for the ladies Flowering Seeds.

Come and See.   Seeing is Believing.

Yours Respectfully, C. D. Stoddard

A newspaper item that appeared on September 13, 1888, informed readers that "C. D. Stoddard says it pays to advertise. Last week he advertised for a girl, and Tuesday night of this week one arrived at his house. She is rather delicate to do general house work yet, but if she keeps her present good health, she will be a big help in a few years." I imagine readers of the *DeWitt Times* quite enjoyed the humorous way of announcing the birth of a child (Lois). Undoubtedly Collins and Nella were very proud of their daughter, who was photographed with her parents a few years later (see Fig. 19).

Fig. 19 Collins and Nella with Lois

Within a few weeks after Lois' birth, the news was less joyful when the newspaper reported that "C. D. Stoddard has decided to close out his entire stock of dry goods and will sell them cheap for cash. They must be sold before the first of the year."

The final move of Collins' multi-stage migration occurred in May of 1889 when the family moved to Sunny Slope Farm. He lived there a little over a decade before his death on the 13th of January 1901.

The following is not an obituary, but in later year Collins' son Hugh summarized his father's life after Collins and Nella were married:

> *Collins was not a good businessman. In his kindness he trusted people too much. His partner took advantage of him and customers failed to pay their bills. He traded his interest in the store for a farm, only to*

find he had been deceived, and had nothing left. In this situation, Nella's parents rented them 51 acres of land with no buildings, but having an open well from which water could be secured with rope and bucket. Grandpa [Benton] would hold this land for her till she could pay for it. With money due Nella for work at home since she was of age, she built a house 20' x 22' without foundation, only wide soft pine floorboards, one partition, only the kitchen plastered, the rest being boxed with boards inside. In the attic were a few loose boards to walk on and to support the beds. The attic was reached by a ladder. Into this the family of six moved in the spring of 1889.

Collins was not a robust man. After years of illness, he died January 13, 1901. By this time the two older children were married and Tom was working away from home. Lois was then 12½, Wayne 8½, and I was 20 months. Collins' personal property was insufficient for the debts, but his membership in the Ancient Order of United Workmen, provided $2,000 life insurance. With this Nella paid for the 51 acres, then worth about twice that. This enabled her through frugality to support herself and three children.

CHAPTER SIX

NELLA ALDRICH

Nella Aldrich, my paternal grandmother, came to Nebraska with her parents when she was almost eight years old. Although she lived a few years in Saline County, Nebraska, and she once seriously considered moving to Colorado, major events in her life brought her to Nemaha County, where she lived most of her long life. This chapter includes portions of her lengthy letters and recollections, all of which reveal her motives for her migratory decisions.

Nella, who was the second child of Benton and Jennie Aldrich, was born the 4th of July 1857 in Wiscoy, Minnesota. According to her accounts, her life as a young child was fairly normal for a Midwestern family at that period of time. In the early 1930s, she recounted some specific memories of her childhood to her daughter-in-law Nainie Stoddard.

Nella remembered having a daguerreotype picture taken when she was five (see Fig. 20). The memory was vivid (because, when her father stepped from the photographer's room, Nella feared he had left her, which consequently affected the pose the photographer sought.

Fig. 20. Nella Aldrich, age 5

She also fondly recalled a pink shirt waist that a doting relative made for her (see Fig. 21). Another early memory involved her mother using a dress to fight a prairie fire.

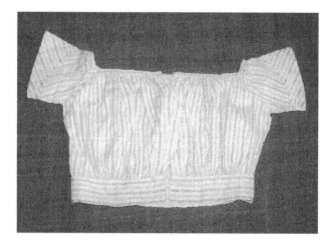

Fig. 21. Nella Aldrich's shirt waist

Nella also recollected witnessing her grandparents' grief when her uncle died (of measles) during the Civil War.

It's not surprising that Nella (when she was almost 8 years old) viewed the family's trip to Nebraska somewhat differently than did her parents (see Chapters 3 & 4). Some of her memories, as dictated to Nainie, follow:

> *Father hauled his corn to Rumsey's Landing, Wis., on the Chippewa River, and sold it. After the corn was sold and he had the pay* [cash] *for it, my parents pulled down the shades to the windows and then Father spread out the gold coins on the table. That sight impressed my mind vividly.*
>
> *Father hired a man to take a load of goods to Wiscoy, Minn., where three of his Farrar cousins lived and where our first home had been. We went in a small sleigh or cutter, drawn by one horse.*
>
> *We made a visit of several weeks with three of Father's cousins, and their families, and neighbors we used to know so well. We made our home with Father's cousin, Levi Farrar, who had bought the home that we had left.*
>
> *In preparing food for our journey, we wanted to be as economical as we could, and my parents used graham flour and made a great quantity of graham crackers, or hard cakes. Levi Farrar's father made these crackers because he thought it too much for Mother, and he had time to use in this way. He rolled his sleeves above his elbows and mixed, kneaded, and rolled the bread. It lasted all the way – till we got to Nebraska.*
>
> *We crossed the Missouri River at Nebraska City, on a ferry boat. At last we were at Nebraska City! We drove quite a little distance on the bottom along the south side of the Nemaha River. Here we saw the grass was several inches high and a rich green. During the six weeks we were on the way, we had traveled south and west so*

many miles and the season had advanced during the time, until we were all glad to see the springtime after the long trip and the winter weather.

The country here was quite different from what I had ever seen before. I had seen bluffs with trees on, and prairie land that was treeless, but these little hills, one after the other, with stony bluffs and little hollows that ran down between the bluffs, with little ponds of water after a rain, were new and interesting to me.

One day while Father was breaking this land, a score or more of Indians – men, women, and children, large and small – and dogs – stopped and talked with Father a short time, and then went farther west of William Hawley's home, and they camped there near the creek, and stayed there a day or two. Karl and I got permission to follow them, and saw them pitch their tents and get settled. The little Indian boys were like ducks, they liked to jump in the water and splash around. Mr. Hawley said it took several days for the water to clear after the Indians left. Mrs. Hawley was quite afraid of the Indians who came up to her house and begged for food for their papooses.

Several days after these Indians left, there was an Indian man and woman, who belonged to the company just previously spoken of, that came to where Father was breaking prairie and stopped and talked a short time with him. The man was walking and the woman was sitting on something of a platform fastened on the pony's back. As I remember it, she sat with her feet curled up on this platform, and I think in her arms was a baby. They were going to overtake these other Indians, as they had stopped a few days when she gave birth to the babe.

Commencing in the summer of 1881, Nella kept a diary in which she often described in detail various events and her feelings about them. Her writings are informative because they probably typify those of a young adult female living in rural eastern Nebraska during the state's early history and because they advance the migratory theme of this book,

Nella's diary shows that, on the one hand, she had a close relationship with her family and the neighborhood in which they lived; she did not want to disturb the accepted norms. On the other hand, she was curious about a wider world and was ready to journey elsewhere where she might encounter new experiences.

When Nella was 24, she went to see a circus and animal show at Nebraska City. She deemed the performance as "wonderful", but she thought it would be her last circus because it seemed to her that "everyone in the country suddenly turned mad" and she "shrank from the thought of being one of them".

In mid-Sept. of the same year Nella went with a group (siblings and neighbors) to attend the Nebraska State Fair in Omaha. From Nebraska City they took a ferry across the Missouri River and boarded a north-bound train. Nella was excited because this was her first train ride. They spent the night in a depot because all the hotels in town were full. Before trying to sleep, they decided to go to a theater. About that event, she wrote: "We did not understand the play very well, but I saw at once it was sensational." After describing the performance, she added: "I had a little experience while at the theatre that is not very pleasant to think of. I was frightened at first but after a moment's reflection acted as I think a virtuous woman should."

During the next few years, Nella suffered a variety of physical problems. In July of 1882 she severely sprained her right ankle. Later when she was running a high fever, she lamented that she was confined to her bed and was growing too weak to walk. She began "to be tired of living" and she wished she "might die in some easy way but did not feel quite brave enough to do so". Her parents called Dr. Larsh of Nebr. City and he pronounced it was "nervous fever or what is more commonly known as lock jaw".

The next May Nella prepared to go to Chicago with friends to see the Columbian Exposition (World's Fair), after which she planned to continue alone to visit her grandparents in Wisconsin. Her comments indicated she was very excited about this upcoming adventure. When she prepared to board the train in Brock, Benton gave the following fatherly advice to his 26-year-old daughter: "If you get in trouble, ask the Conductor or a Policeman. If you get out of money have some one telegraph us – tell your story; someone will help you. A hotel keeper will not turn you away – you can go to work!"

On the 9th of June 1883, Nella and friends did attend the Fair. She obviously was very impressed by stores in Chicago and the technology of the Fair. She reported:

> We went first to the largest dry goods store west of New York City, kept by Marshall Field & Co. It is a very large building; 4 stories high; three for goods & the upper is all used for making & cutting garments. We went up on the elevator but walked down. We went to several dry goods stores & in one I saw the new cash system where the money is carried in balls that roll in a wire race from one end of the building to the other. We tarried a few moments in several other places & went to the exposition building. It would be difficult to numerate the things of interest I saw there. I had as good a sight of the electric lights as is possible in day time where the rooms are partially darkened from the sun. [N.B. Powering the Fair with electricity had become a "War of Currents" involving DC vs. AC electricity, General Electric vs. Westinghouse as supplier, and a variety of competing types of lamps.]

Nella did not complete her planned itinerary because her grandmother had become ill so Nella was instructed to return home.

In the fall of 1886 Nella again sprained her right ankle. When it did not seem to heal, she took the train from Johnson to Nebraska City to see Dr. Larsh. By the time she reached his home, she was weak from a "lack of food", the "tedious journey", and "difficulty in getting a ride from the depot to the Dr. residence". After arriving at the doctor's home, she introduced herself, and asked Mrs. Larsh "the privilege of lying on the sofa." Dr. Larsh soon came into the room and examined Nella. She wrote that he thought "I was starving myself & that I must eat fresh beef, eggs, cheese, & milk." She immediately followed his directions and "ate the first mouthful of meat that noon Sept. 10th 1886 at 29 yrs. of age". It is undeniable that Nella regarded her decision to follow the doctor's instructions as significant event in her life at that time. He also gave her some medicine, which she declared was acidic.

After she sprained her wrist in March 1887, Nella went to see Dr. Oppermann in Auburn. He wrapped her wrist, as well as her ankle, with a rubber bandage; and he gave her a bottle of what she called "skunk's oil" to apply on the two sprains.

Nella gradually recuperated from these injuries and was ready for new adventures, a major one being a decision to go to Colorado to take out a homestead. She listed several reasons why she thought this would be a wise move: her doctor thought she needed a change of place, her mother and Karl thought it would be a "fine thing" to have land of her own, and she wanted "to do more for myself than I could do here" (that is, in Nemaha County).

What would have been the outcome if she had fulfilled her plans to migrate to Colorado? The answer is unknown, because before she had packed and left, she received a letter from C.D. Stoddard. That letter completely changed the direction of her life.

In that letter, which redirected the trajectory of both of their lives, C.D. (Collins) told about the death of his wife and the need for a mother of his three children (see Chapter 5). Her response follows:

> *Mr. Stoddard*   *Brock Nemaha Co. Nebr.*
> *Dear Friend:*   *July 3rd 1887*
> *I can hardly express my surprise at the contents of your letter. So unlooked for from any one, and much less from one whom I have not seen or heard from for so many years. I sympathize deeply with you in your bereavement.*

I am unmarried yet and will accept your invitation to correspond. It has been long since we have met, and I was so much younger then, that I feel as if we are almost strangers, yet what I do remember of you is very favorable.

I am sorry to say that I have been in ill health for the past two years, but it is improving now and am in hopes I shall be well again.

I infer from the stamp on your letter that you live in DeWitt and follow the mercantile business. Am I correct?

Prosperity to you and yours, Sincerely,   Nella Aldrich

The "courtship" correspondence makes a poignant read, particularly because Nella shared her apprehension, as well as her determination, about many issues. Here I have excluded most of what she wrote, but retained some sections that I believe convey several of her salient characteristics. Two of her letters, written soon after her acknowledgment of his letter of July 3rd, are the following:

July 11, 1887. Permit me to ask one favor of you. Please don't put your name and address on your envelopes – our hired men and neighbors often bring our mail from the office and I don't want them to know anything yet about my new friend.

July 28, 1887. It troubles me to hear of your loneliness. I had hoped that your visit had the same effect upon you that it did upon me. Since that eventful ride to the lake, I have passed the happiest hours that I have known for five years. I feel now that it is all settled and that, if we were truthful to each other, as I believe we were, then nothing but death will prevent us from walking down life's pathway together. With this thought and the planning for the future, knowing there is someone not far away who is so devoted to me, is quite enough for a while. Can you not feel the same?

What transpired at "the lake", it seems, was essentially an engagement. Certainly the letters of the next several weeks indicate that the courtship had matured enough that they began expressing some of their differences. One related to the time of marriage. Collins was eager to marry immediately, but Nella was reluctant to marry too soon after he had become a widower. As she stated: "Perhaps I have too much pride and care too much for the good opinion of others." Her concern about how the community would view her family is exposed in another letter, which clearly reflects the views of her father Benton: "If we common people are honest & just & are careful to associate with those of our kind, we should be content."

Another factor that made Nella reluctant to marry immediately was her medical condition. In a letter to Collins in early September, she reported on what her doctor told her:

He advised me again as he had many times before to get married; he says that Nature's cure of the disease is the bearing of children, the only one in some cases. He says that is the natural function of that organ & and the nonuse tends to weaken the contractions of all of the muscles. [The next day Nella wrote:] *I am feeling quite badly again today. My Dear, I have feared of late that I will slowly grow worse until I am so weak that some acute disease will end my suffering, and that we shall never be more than lovers. It seems as if I could not bear to have my life end thus. Perhaps I should not entertain such thoughts, but one symptom of this disease is despondency. Did you ever know of any one as I am who became permanently better? I do not expect to entirely recover. I told Mother that other day that I pitied you with all my heart with falling in love with such a worthless creature.*

It appears that, within a week, Nella viewed life much more optimistically and was ready to consider a marriage date. Even so, she remained concerned about the proper waiting time before marriage, as well as the propriety of the circumstances of the ceremony. The following indicates some issues that were on her mind:

> *I much prefer to be married at home. Several girls in our neighborhood have married against their parents' consent or even without their knowledge. Now I am thinking about what people will say again, but really I do not want anyone to think I have lived these years single & then married unwisely or without my parents' consent.*
>
> *Some* [members] *of my family think that it would look better* [if you obtained the marriage license in person]. *Father should meet you at the Court House* [then after you get the license, the two of you can come to our home.] *We should be married just after lamp lighting.*
>
> *I am aware that we care for looks more than you do, but I believe my marriage & leaving home so suddenly will be a great surprise to many & I wish to have it done so there will be no chance of suspicion of any kind.*

The wedding of Nella and Collins was on Oct. 6th, 1887. They immediately took the train to DeWitt, where they commenced their married life (see Fig. 22). In a letter Nella sent to a friend a few days later, she summarized the events that led to her marriage and wrote that "I have a pleasant home" and that "I like living in a small village better than I thought would be the case".

Fig. 22 Nella Aldrich Stoddard, 1887

After her marriage, Nella did not keep a personal diary. As noted in Chapter 5, Collins sold his store at the end of 1888. On the 5th of May, the family made a final more to Sunny Slope Farm, where Nella lived the rest of her life. I am sorry she did not share her thoughts relating to the health and eventual death of her husband. In fact, the only information about that period is what Benton wrote, which is the following:

> *Since* [Collins' death], *she and her children have lived alone, renting the plow land and managing the rest herself. As there were more girls than boys in my family in her young days, she learned by much practice to do farm work, so now, having fifty acres of land, her "trade" enables her to do some things and to oversee others.*

By the time of Collins' death, Nella's three stepchildren had left home so she devoted her attentions to the well-being of Lois, Wayne, and Hugh (Figs. 23).

Fig. 23 Wayne, Lois, Hugh, 1901

Even after the three gained adulthood (Fig. 24), the interaction among them and their mother was close.

Fig. 24 Nella Stoddard with Lois, Wayne, and Hugh

All three remained on Nella's portion of the "Aldrich" land, with Nella, Lois, and Hugh jointly farming one part, while Wayne became the owner of another segment.

Nella was very much attached to her home place. She was constantly busy with household and gardening tasks, and she expressed dissatisfaction with being "idle" (see Fig. 25).

Fig. 25. Nella Stoddard, 1930

Although she seldom left home, she did venture forth a couple times to visit relatives. The first one was to Boise, Idaho (in 1922) to meet with a descendant of Mattie. A decade later she took another a trip (this time by car with Lois) to visit places memorable to her life in Minnesota.

During Nella's lifetime she experienced several technological inventions. Rather than traveling by animal power and trains, she had the convenience of auto power in her later years; and although she had observed the use of electricity when she was in Chicago in 1883, it was not until more than three-quarters of a century later (when she was in her "senior years") that she was able to reap its benefits. Some of these are described by Lois in her diary:

We have electricity in our home [as a result of the
Government's Rural Electrification Act]. *My first thot
was for an electric refrigerator. That would save us
from six to twelve trips to the basement each day, where
the food was not cool enuf when the weather was hot.
We now have an electric refrigerator in our pantry. We
also have an electric washing machine.*

One morning a few months later, Lois realized her mother was
having trouble eating breakfast. Later when the doctor came, he
diagnosed the problem as a slight paralytic stroke. Soon Nella seemed
to recover well enough that she wanted to resume doing "her share of
work" by fulfilling what she regarded as her obligation to the family
welfare. In fact, Nella insisted that Lois assign some tasks which she
could do. However, a few days later – the 24th of December 1938 – she
died peacefully in her home on the land she dearly loved.

CHAPTER SEVEN

THEODORE HENRY ROBERTSON

One of my great grandfathers on my mother's ancestral tree was Theodore Henry Robertson (familiarly called T.H.). As was the case for my other great grandparents, several generations of T.H.'s forebears were in America for many decades prior to the nineteenth century.

The father of T.H. was John Bouden (J.B.) Robertson. Several of J.B.'s ancestors worked in iron mills, as did many Scottish immigrants in the late eighteenth century. In fact, J.B. worked as an iron molder in the Cuyahoga Steam Furnace for a period of time.

The mother of T.H. was Temperance (Tempa) Foote. One of her great grandfathers had lived in the Plymouth Colony. Her early life was summarized in the melodramatic obituary that follows:

> Mrs. Robertson was of the good old puritan stock. Her first ancestors to arrive in America landed here in 1616, and settled in Massachusetts, where they with others endured the hardships and privations incident to a settlement amidst unbroken forests inhabited by both savage men and beasts.
>
> Mrs. Robertson was born when the swiftest means of travel on land was what it had been thousands of

years – horse power – and that upon water what it had been during all the past –wind power. Her memory went back to the time when the first steam boat floated upon the waters of our or any other country and she has lived to see the most distant nations of the earth become neighbors through the wide spread and vast development of that principle applied to navigation.

She could easily remember where the first railroad train started out to demonstrate that steam was cheaper and better than horse power for travel and transportation.

She was nearly in her prime when the first attempts were made to control electricity and compel it to do our bidding and she lived to be able through its wonderful power to learn all the great changes, transactions and accidents of the world within twenty-four hours of their happening and through the wonderful progress in gathering and printing news to get all for a penny.

J.B. and Tempa married in Lee, Massachusetts, in 1821, but they soon left because of "a lawsuit" (the nature of which is unknown to me). They moved to a farm at Rockport, Ohio; but a couple of years later, they sold the Rockport farm and moved to a farm in Amherst Township, Lorain Co., Ohio. Tempa lived the rest of her life on their farm in Ohio; but she was very involved with the life of family members in faraway Nebraska (see more below).

Why J.B. initially moved to Nebraska was not recorded by any of the documents I found; and even the exact date of his arrival is vague. It may have been about 1854 because local newspapers announced that in that year he served as a Judge of Elections in Burt County. In any case, his presence in eastern Nebraska is documented by the fact that he was one of the two members from that county to the House of Representatives of the first Nebraska Territorial Legislature. Furthermore, a newspaper reported that one of the two voting places in Burt County was "at the house of Gen. John B. Robertson".

J.B.'s legislative role was significant because the Kansas-Nebraska Act of 1854 had just created the Nebraska Territory, an act that led to the need for convening a territorial legislature to administer the hitherto unorganized territory. The responsibilities placed on the legislators were great, even though the facilities were quite minimal and the competency of many members was limited. The Legislature met in a newly built two-story brick building in the new town of Omaha. Legislators sat at school desks, with two at each desk. The next year J.B. was appointed Quartermaster of the First Regiment of the Nebraska Militia, which may have been the reason "Gen." was sometimes attached to his name.

Later that year J.B. commenced his service to the Omaha tribe as "Indian Farmer". While in that service, he wrote numerous letters and reports to the Commissioner of Indian Affairs in St. Louis (all of which are stored on microfilm in the library of the Nebraska State Historical Society). These documents reveal his attempts to convert the Omaha into tillers of the soil and his frustration with the Omahas' priority for hunting. In his reports, he often wrote lengthy explanations about his relations with the Omaha, about disputes with government officials in the field, and about various financial matters.

For this book, I have chosen only a few that may typify J.B.'s view of matters and his way of communicating them (including his spelling and grammar). The first, which was written on the 1st of October 1855, follows:

> *The Omahas are now located on the north side of the Platt about 15 miles from this place, where they have been since there return from there hunt, where Logan Fontenelle & others were killed by the Sioux. I was at that time engaged by the agent in opening there farm at Black Bird, where I succeeded in breaking about one hundred & forty acres and putting in crops to a considerable amt.*
>
> *There not returning to Black Bird but insisting to remain on the Platt, I felt it my duty to reside as near them as I could. My residence at Black Bird has convinced me of the value to the Indians of that location*

as it abounds with game & fish and will when brought in cultivation become valuable for farming purposes To which in my opinion should their attention be turned as fast as possible.

I have recently, in company with Indian Agent Hepner, paid a visit to the Pawnees at there Village on the South of the Platt. We had a talk with them concerning their selling their land to the Government.

On July 22, 1856, J.B. gave the Commissioner the following account of his "transactions with the Indians":

As farmer for the Omahas I went to work as early a day as practicable last spring at the reserve at Black Bird Hills, and am happy to be able to inform you that my survey both as to the extent and prospects of the crops, fully equal my most genuine expectations.

I got in about one hundred acres of corn and potatoes, which is mostly secured by good fences, has been cultivated, and looks thrifty and promising. Quite a number of Indians expressed a determination to apply themselves more to agriculture, and in working the present crop, have given encouraging proof to the truth of what they say.

Though somewhat disappointed in not securing a payment during the past spring, they left on there usual hunt about the 10th instant, satisfied with the hope of a double payment about the first of September next, at which time they will return.

It may come within the sphere of my duty to appraise you that agent Hepner and myself selected a place last fall for the agency building and Indian mills. The place selected was every way the most eligible we could find on the Reserve. During the past spring the Rev. Mr. Hamilton selected the same place for the Mission

*School and is going on to improve it for that purpose,
notwithstanding I notified him of our prior selection.*

In August 1856, J.B. was promoted to the position of Indian Agent
by the Northern-Democratic Presidential Administration. Receiving
that governmental position is not surprising because J.B. was an
active Democratic politician. he was already living in the Nebraska
Territory, and he knew the Omaha because of his former position
as Indian Farmer. His first report as Agent, which he sent to the
Commissioners of Indian Affairs on September 8th, is the following:

> *I arrived at this place on the evening of the 24th ult.,
> and learned that the Indians attached to this Agency
> had not returned from their hunt.*
>
> *The agricultural implements, and all the property
> pertaining to the farm, except the team and wagon,
> were purchased by myself, for most of which I am still
> individually liable, as they were bought on credit during
> the suspension of Agent Hepner, with the understanding
> that there were funds in his hands, with which to pay
> for them. I find the Agency in debt about three thousand
> dollars, which debts were contracted by Ag't Hepner
> before his suspension for breaking up and fencing the
> prairie, and by Agent Vanderslyce for erecting buildings,
> etc., and for farming utensils by myself, while acting
> under the orders of Agents Hepner and Vanderslyce.*

In the spring of 1858, J.B. was asked to escort a delegation of Ponca
chiefs to Washington, D.C., for the purpose of having them cede most
of their Nebraska land. The event was publicized in an article with
an engraved picture in *Frank Leslie's Illustrated Newspaper* (see Fig.
26), which guaranteed wide exposure because of the publication's
popularity. [N.B. *Leslie's Weekly* – as it was commonly called –
printed pictures of many national events for several decades during
the late 19th century.]

Fig. 26. J. B. Robertson (third from the left back row) with Ponca Chiefs

Undoubtedly the article that accompanied the picture reflects the popular cultural attitudes of the day and was written to attract readers. A portion of that news items states:

No. 124, Vol. V New York, Saturday, April 17, 1858 Price 6 Cents Delegation of Chiefs From the Poncah Tribe of Nebraska Indians

The appearance of this Nebraska tribe in the streets of the national metropolis and in our own city was picturesque, and suggested novel speculation. On the one side was civilization, represented by the passing, busy, thoughtful crowd; on the other side was barbarism, displayed in the grandest form, in the persons of hostile tribes decked out in their wild and striking costumes – their red and blue blankets wrapped closely around them; their long straight black locks stuck full of eagle plumes, bound together by uncouth headgear of all shapes, colors and modes of manufacture; their ears over laden with ponderous rings; their necks adorned with necklaces of bears claws, artistically wrought together; their breasts and shoulders slashed with the scalps which they had taken from their enemies; their hands grasping the spear, tomahawk and the war club; and their faces, and sometimes their hair daubed over with masses of red, blue, green and yellow paint, disposed in fantastic forms and patterns, in accordance with the rules of the only heraldry – such as it is – to which they are accustomed, and which amongst them is as much subject to the law and ordinance of hereditary descent as the heraldry of griffins, boars' heads, lions rampant and bloody hands so common in the coat of arms shops in Europe, and, we blush to say, not totally unknown in Republic America.

The Poncah chiefs were five in number, fierce, stalwart, but melancholy-looking men, with natural dignity impressed upon their features and glancing from their eyes. They are all without exception powerful men, standing six feet high, and very muscular.

The chiefs were accompanied by J. B. Robertson, agent of the tribe, Henry Fontenelle, United States Interpreter, and Francis Roy, interpreter of the tribe.

J.B.'s position as Indian Agent ended in the summer of 1858. The *Nebraska City News* informed its readers of that event when it wrote that "Gen. J.B. Robertson has been removed from the office of Indian Agent".

I have not found documentation about the reason for the "removal" of J.B. as Indian Agent to the Omaha. To speculate about explanations for his "removal" is very risky because (a) the event occurred during an earlier cultural climate when attitudes and behaviors sometimes differed from those of today, (b) civil servants held varying views about how to implement government policies, and (c) individual personalities resulted in diverse behavior.

After being terminated as Indian Agent, J.B. returned to his Ohio farm where he and his wife Tempa lived the rest of their lives. They had six children, with T.H., their third child, being born in March 1824.

The rest of this chapter recounts the fascinating life of my great grandfather (T. H.) rather than on my great great grandfather (J.B).

T.H. studied to be a lawyer; but evidently he did not practice much, even though he was an appointed member of the American Legal Association and later was admitted to the Bar in Lorain County, Ohio. However, the diary T.H. kept in 1849 indicates he spent much of his time teaching school. His diary also reveals that he had a great interest in politics – and enjoyed a dry humor, as expressed in some of the following selected entries:

> *Monday, January 1ˢᵗ 1849. Went to Elyria the first time for a month. I have now been teaching school at Amherstville for four weeks. My health is poor and the school is large. Indeed at times I think I had about as lief die as live were it not for the uncertain contingencies of the hereafter.*
>
> *Saturday 27 Jan. Had a lawsuit to attend in Black River before Mr. Harris, but got the case adjourned for the purpose of getting testimony.*
>
> *Monday 5 Mar. Received my money for teaching, or fifty dollars of it, and attended the ball at Steeles, which, all things considering, went off very well. The company however was of a mixed nature, all the very streaked and specked being there.*
>
> *Sunday 18 Mar. I had quite a long conversation with Miss Crocker at her own request. This was the first private conversation we had had since engagement was broken off, which took place the last day of December last. She feels quite bad and judging from appearances would like very well to make up with me again; but I thought I cannot but feel some pity for one who has acted so foolishly. The sacred relation of man and wife is too important for me to peril my happiness in this world thus lightly by reinstating my affections for one who has once acted the part of a coquette.*

Friday 29 June. Have read about 30 pages of Law, and written one or two declarations.

There were 83 deaths by Cholera reported in yesterday's papers in Cincinnati; what an awful Scourge this pestilence is to the human family and how mysterious its progress, commencing in one quarter of the world and continuing its progress until it has entirely encircled the globe. In to-day's papers 150 deaths by Cholera are reported in Cincinnati within the last twenty four hours. [See Explanatory Panel "Cholera in Ohio in 1849"].

Cholera in Ohio in 1849

Cholera first appeared in the United States in 1832, probably brought by European immigrants. Cleveland residents were the first people in Ohio to contract the illness, but the disease soon spread to other parts of the state, such as Cincinnati on the Ohio River. With poor sanitation systems, cholera tended to be most virulent in cities, but it also occurred along canals with their stagnant waters.

The worst epidemic to affect Ohio occurred in 1849. Eight thousand people in Cincinnati died in this epidemic, including Harriet Beecher Stowe's infant son. Panic led many Cincinnati residents to flee the city for areas less densely populated. Former President James Polk, a resident of Tennessee, was the most famous person to die of cholera in 1849. On Aug. 3rd, T.H. Robertson noted in his diary that Pres. Zachery Taylor designated the day as one of fasting, humiliation, and prayer.

Monday 31 Dec. The last day of December and consequently the middle of the 19th century. And it being such, it behooves us to inquire what has been done in the line of improvements since the commencement of the year 1800. The power of propelling boats and carriages by steam has come into vogue and general use. The magnetic telegraph has been invented and now, instead of being obliged to wait three or four weeks for the answer to a communication sent one or two hundred miles, we can send a communication more than one thousand miles and get an answer in less time than one hour. We have turnpikes, plank roads, and McAdamized roads and canals and rail roads to travel on instead of the miserably constructed and dreary roads of fifty years since. [N. B. Macadam was a type of road promoted by the Scotsman John McAdam in about 1820, which had a subgrade of crushed stone overlaid with a surface of light stone that would absorb wear and tear and shed water.] *Instead of the clumsy wagons and old scows for the lakes, we now have light and neatly constructed carriages for the roads and steamers, with nicely furnished cabins and rooms for the waters; and the distance that required three weeks to traverse is now very easily accomplished in three days or even less.*

This question then naturally presents itself to the thinking mind. If society continues to improve for the coming fifty years in the same ratio they have for the last and their improvements are as extensive, to what a stage of civilization and convenience will we have arrived? What improvements can be made that are not already in perfection? I think there is some room for that in our carriages, and perhaps some mastermind will invent a way by which railroad cars can be made to travel at the rate of 100 miles per hour.

I found it very revealing about humankind's history of inventions when I read this in T.H.'s 1849 diary. What he speculated about possible improvements in carriages and the speed of trains pales in comparison with today's modes of transportation and explorations of space.

In March 1854, T.H. married Julia Johnson, and their daughter Fannie was born a year later. I do not have a picture of either Julia or Fannie, but I have one of TH. (see Fig. 27.)

Fig. 27 Theodore Henry Robertson

Soon afterwards T.H. made a major decision – one that brought him to Nebraska and changed the trajectory of his life. A strong rationale could be made that the reason for moving to eastern Nebraska was that his father J.B. was already there (see above); but that does not completely explain why T.H. even wanted to leave his home in Lorrain County.

I am uncertain about the exact date T.H. moved to Sarpy County, Nebraska, but the author of his obituary wrote that the family came in early 1856. Whatever the case, T.H. soon jumped into the fray of politics. He had always been very interested in politics, but the issues of the 1850s and 1860s associated with the American Civil War generated heated debates. Because of his fractious personality, it is not surprising that he was soon deeply involved with the political controversies of Nebraska.

The politics prior to, during, and immediately following the Civil War were so complex it is impossible to adequately characterize the many political factions; nevertheless, it might be helpful when reading about T.H. to note some information about Nebraska and national factions that erupted in verbal and written clashes (see Explanatory Panel "Early Nebraska Politics").

Early Nebraska Politics

Most Nebraskans in the late 1850s and early 1860s were against slavery, but the issue split the parties. The first meeting of the Republican Party in the state was in 1858, but only a few persons attended and were called "Black Republicans". In some counties they combined with Democrats and called their ticket the "people's ticket". The national Democratic Party was split between the hardline pro-slavery Southerners, who nominated John C. Breckinridge for the 1860 presidential slate, and the more moderate group, who nominated Stephen A. Douglas.

A prominent Republican in Nebraska was Robert W. Furnas, who was elected governor in 1872. A major Nebraska Democratic figure was Experience Estabrook, who was appointed attorney general of the Territory of Nebraska in 1855 and served as Delegate-elect for the Territory 1859-60. Another well-known figure of the day was J. Sterling Morton, who served briefly in the Nebraska Territorial House of Representatives (1855-56), the Secretary of the Territory (1858-61), and Acting Governor (1858-59). He declared himself as a Douglas Democrat because of the general anti-slavery feelings in the Territory.

T. H. became editor (and later part owner) of *The Nebraskian* (later known as the *Omaha Nebraskian)*, the first newspaper printed in Omaha (i.e., other newspapers were available in the city in 1856, but they were published elsewhere). As editor, he had a ready avenue for publicizing his strong opinions, many of which provoked commentaries in other newspapers. What follows are editorials from the *Nebraska City News*, and the *Brownville Advertiser*, and of course from the *Omaha Nebraskian* that give a flavor of the printed invectives of that time:

> January 9, 1858. [*Nebraska City News*] T.H. Robertson, the reputed and ostensible Editor of the *Nebraskian* has been expelled from his seat as reporter in the Nebraska Legislature: reason, "abuse of privilege". How he was ever admitted is a profound mystery to us.

> July 26, 1860. [*Nebraska Advertiser*] Complimentary. T.H. Robertson, of the *Omaha Nebraskian,* familiarly known in this country as the sycophantic spaniel owned by whoever may be in official position about him; who was expelled as a reporter from within the bar of the Nebraska Legislature, for his low, vulgar course towards members; who was publicly cowhided by a lady, on the Post Office steps, in his own town, for his insolence, and blackguardism, and who is characterized wherever known, as being the most dishonest, knavish, foul-mouthed, slippery, unscrupulous, treacherous, false-hearted, cowardly, groveling, scurvy, beggarly, dishonorable, ungentlemanly, recreant, undignified, uncivilized, boorish, obnoxious, insignificant, trifling, vulgar, insolent, impertinent, egotistical, base, servile, supple, cringing, fawning, growling, parasitical, and abject mass of putridity, ever by mistake, wrapped in human hide, pays us the following compliment:

>> "R. W. Furnas, of the *Brownville Advertiser,* familiarly known in days past as 'Bob,' whose fondness for fobbing legislative gratuities is proverbial, and whose treachery to the part to which he professed allegiance last year is

notorious, has at last gone over, body, soul and breeches to the Black Republicans."

We say complimentary, because it is a compliment to be abused by Robertson. We had much rather he would speak ill of us than favorably.

His praise would make any honest man feel as though he had been guilty of stealing sheep, or acorns from a blind hog.

July 26, 1860. [*Nebraska Advertiser*] Old Fashioned Morality and Virtue. The *Nebraskian*, in commenting upon our article and course, in prefering [sic] the election of Lincoln and Hamlin to that of Breckinridge and Lane, bids us "an affectionate good-bye" and talks of morality and virtue!

Ye Gods!!! From a personal knowledge of the man, his habits and instincts, we are safe in concluding that the "old fashioned notions of morality and virtue," of Robertson, are co-equal with those practices by such "old fashioned," worthies as Judas, Cain, Eve, Lot's daughters, the rabble who cried "Away with him! Crucify him! Crucify him!"

The Omaha Nebraskian was full of editorial comments by T.H. throughout this period; but here I have included only the three he wrote in 1860:

July 28,1860. [*Omaha Nebraskian*] Remember! That Stephen A. Douglas is the only Presidential candidate who will receive votes in every State of this Union. Remember, too, that Stephen A. Douglas will be the next President of the United States. He never has been beaten, and his star will certainly not begin to wane in 1860. The people are with him!

Nov. 17, 1860. [*Omaha Nebraskian*] The Election and Its Results. Lincoln is elected. For evil or for good, the die is cast; and we have lived to witness, in this once powerful and happy confederacy, a sectional party triumph. We have seen, we cannot express with how much regret, a morbid feeling for an abstract and false idea about the ubiquitous nigger, override every consideration of respect for the Constitution of the United States, and for the rights, happiness and safety of twenty millions of our race; children of the men who redeemed this land from the savage, and won its liberty from Great Britain. We have beheld the final act that completes the alienation of the hearts of this people from the confederacy, by a geographical line. The Union still stands, but the loyalty, respect, esteem and mutual affection that made its chief beauty and strength, have perished before our very eyes.

Dec. 22, 1860. [*Omaha Nebraskian*] Muzzling the Press. A resolution to exclude us from a seat within the bar, on Monday last passed the Council by a vote of seven to five – every Republican but one voting in the affirmative. The Council has ordered the Sergeant-at-arms to prevent our entrance within the bar of that Hall, but we would not change positions with a single member who voted for that resolution. The editor of a paper like ours occupies an infinitely higher place in the estimation of mankind, than the infinitesimal intellects that obeyed the beck of a master whose friendship is dishonest and whose name is a synonym for infamy. We feel honored by the action of that body, but mortified and chagrined that the Territory should be disgraced with Legislators who connive at, and sanction infamous election frauds, and whose highest ambition is to convert the Council Chamber into a pot house debating club, for the discussion of personal spite, petty malice, and imaginary grievances – employing in such discussions ribald language and low slang, that would disgrace a convocation of fish-market women. There are, in this world of ours, hideous toads, that spit venom at all who offend them; and some men, we regret to say, are toads by instinct. If by chance some such bipeds occupy seats in that Council, the misfortune is the Territory's, not ours; who never aided in their election.

> This action of the Council, weighs not a feather in our mind, and these remarks are dictated by no other emotions than pity for the poor creatures who so forgot their duty as legislators, as to make themselves ridiculous if not infamous by a puerile attempt to stifle the honest sentiment of the press. In conclusion we have to say, that if these remarks be thought too severe, that Council is at liberty to adopt a resolution excluding us from the grounds of the Capitol – if that be not sufficient, we would suggest the propriety of instructing the Sergeant-at-arms to prevent us from walking the streets or entering our own office – if that fails, an edict of perpetual banishment had better be issued forthwith.

The life of T.H. changed dramatically within the next few years: he sold the *Omaha Nebraskian,* his wife died, and he remarried. I do not know why T.H. left the newspaper profession. The letters between T.H. and his new wife (Harriet or "Hattie") during the two years he was in Colorado (see the correspondence later in this chapter and in Chapter Eight) contain occasional hints that suggest they both regretted his disassociation from a newspaper. In any case, the result was that T.H. never returned to the newspaper business.

Julia, T.H.'s first wife and mother of their daughter Fannie, died January 19, 1860. One obituary (evidently authored by T.H.) in *The Omaha Nebraskian* follows:

> With an aching head, eyes blinded with tears, and a heart crushed and overladen with grief, we attempt to pen a few lines. Our heart sinks beneath its great load of grief. A prattling child of five years sits on our knee and in piteous tones asks for her mother, that that mother, the partner of our bosom, lying cold and still. One week ago, she was by our side in good health and with high hopes for the future. Five short days of untold anguish, and she breathed her last, in six days is in the tomb.

After her mother's death, Fannie was returned to Ohio to live with her Robertson grandmother. Fannie was a feisty youngster who loved being back in her original home area; but she also wanted her father to join her there. In a letter dated Aug.17, 1860, T.H.'s mother (Tempa) wrote about how joyously Fannie received letters from her Papa and how much she wished he would return to Lorrain County. Furthermore, she accepted the fact that her mother was dead and she insisted that her father get another wife.

T.H. did, indeed, get another wife: Harriet A. Hogeboom. They married in Larimer (see Explanatory Panel "Larimer"), Sarpy County, Nebraska Territory, on February 11, 1861.

Larimer

The site that became known as Larimer, originally selected by an agent of the American Fur Company in 1854, was located at the junction of the Platte and Missouri rivers. A town was established in 1855 by four men, one being Col. R. Hogaboom and a second being Gen. W. Larimer. Initially a dominant feature of the town was a steam saw that served the region, but soon (1870) this young village gained importance by its connection with the Omaha & Southwestern Railroad network.

Larimer was also called Larimer City and Larimer Mills, until the U.S. Post Office changed the name to La Platte in 1863 because of confusion with Laramie, Wyoming. Although the core of present-day La Platte is not where Larimer was sited, it is in close proximity. La Platte Cemetery, where many members of the Robertson family are buried, is in the same general vicinity.

One of the early public buildings in La Platte was the Stone Hall of 1869, built of native limestone quarried from west of town. Although its early function is not fully documented, it served as a school house at one time. For many years this building (called the Old Stone School) was where the Robertson families held annual reunions during Memorial Day weekends.

Immediately after their wedding, T.H. and Harriet (usually called "Hattie") left for Iowa and Ohio to visit friends and relatives, including Fannie. (Their individual descriptions of that trip are chronicled in Chapter 8.) The newlyweds and Fannie had no more than arrived back home in Nebraska before T.H. left for the gold fields of Colorado.

The correspondence between T.H. and Hattie while he was in the Colorado Territory reveals their agony over being separated during the early years of their marriage. It also exposes their legal and financial problems, as well as their playful humor. Extractions from only a small portion of what T.H. wrote follow:

> *18 June 1861, from Kearney City.*
> *Here we crossed Wood River yesterday evening &*
> *swimming our horses and giving a man a dollar to take*
> *our things across dry in a skiff–the Platte being higher*
> *than it has been earlier this year.*

> *23 June 1861, from Camp No. 11, two miles East of*
> *Julesburg*
> *The romance of the "Great Platte Valley"– about*
> *which I have innocently and ignorantly wrote so much*
> *as a journalist – above Fort Kerny [sic] is effectually*
> *exploded. Not a tree, not a shrub to be seen, no*
> *vegetation but buffalo grass, cactus, and a few – to*
> *me – unknown flowers. The soil is chiefly gravel and*
> *sand strongly imbued with alkali. It can never be made*
> *available as farming or grazing country; it is in fact so*
> *barren, that were it not for the dead carcasses of cattle*
> *& horses, that leave their bones to bleach on the plains,*
> *a buzzard could never fly over it without carrying a*
> *knapsack.*
> *The overland mail companies are doubling their*
> *stations – building half way between those already*
> *constructed. They are putting on a daily line to Salt*
> *Lake. We yesterday passed a large train – 17 coaches,*
> *5 or six hacks, a number of freight wagons and over a*

*hundred mules, belonging to this company and going
out to stock the road beyond Julesburg.*

*With an eye to business, I yesterday stopped about
12 miles back where they are erecting a new station,
and enquired if I could sell them a bill of lumber. They
thought I could if I would sell cheap enough.*

*We have met 3,000 or over Sioux Indians going
to find work about Cottonwood and breathing direst
vengeance against the Pawnees. Their small war party
was unsuccessful in the recent raid against that tribe,
say they found "heap too many Pawnees", and that the
Whites about Columbus helped the latter tribe. They
were very friendly towards us but said they were soon
going on another war party – a larger one – against the
Pawnee, and that they intended to wipe out that tribe and
take the scalps of the White Settlers about Columbus.
I told one of their chiefs, that we cared nothing for the
Pawnees, but if they disturbed a single white person,
General Harney would come out to see them. His reply
was a single "wangh" [?], and the subject was dropped.*

The relations among various Euro-American groups and several
Indian tribes on the Plains were complex (see Explanatory Panel
"Native Americans on the Plains"). Other than that brief encounter at
Camp No. 11, east of Julesburg, T.H. did not comment on any direct
experiences with Native Americans.

Native Americans on the Plains

Native Americans on the American Great Plains during the 19th century were as diverse as the Euro-Americans elsewhere on the continent. Not only were they divided into various tribal groups who ranged over vague and shifting areas, but they differed in their outlooks. Just as the states of eastern United States were fighting a bitter Civil War, several tribes fought each other. For example, the Lakota/Sioux warred against the Pawnee, an antagonism that was acerbated when the latter became scouts for the U.S. Army and protected railroad workers from raids by other tribes. Furthermore, within these groups individuals disagreed about how to settle differences, with some insisting on killing their enemies while others believed in negotiating differences.

Conflicts between Euro-Americans and Native Americans increased dramatically when thousands of gold seekers traveled through the plains in mid-century. In the Fort Laramie Treaty of 1851, the U.S. government recognized the sovereign rights of the Cheyenne and Arapahoe over the territory between the North Platte River and Arkansas River and from the Rocky Mountains to western Kansas. As conflicts during the next several years continued to increase, the territorial officials asked the federal government to sign a more restrictive treaty. Consequently, in February 1861 Cheyenne and Arapaho chiefs ceded all their land in the Treaty of Fort Wise, except for a small area between the Arkansas River and Sand Creek where about a thousand Cheyenne and Arapaho lived. However, some bands of Cheyenne joined the Dog Soldiers (a militaristic band of Cheyenne and Lakota/Sioux) in declaring that the Wise Treaty had not been negotiated legitimately.

Various conflicts, sometimes triggered by minor disputes between a few Euro-Americans and small tribal bands, often escalated into deadly skirmishes when fueled by those seeking retaliation. Several had roots intertwined with the American Civil War, as illustrated by the conflict between the secessionist Texas Confederate and the fighters led by Col. Chivington, the ardent abolitionist preacher. As a result of local political divisions, more than one hundred Arapaho were slaughtered during the infamous Sand Creek Massacre.

One episode was when a group of more militant Sioux, Arapaho, and Cheyenne killed Euro-American civilians and soldiers at Julesburg, Colorado – just five weeks after T.H. had been in that area.

Most of the major massacres – by native tribes or government troops – did not occur along the trails that T.H. frequented. Even though he made several trips between Denver and Omaha, he never expressed apprehension about his safely. However, his outlook may not have been typical of many Euro-Americans at that time.

The rest of the June 23rd letter from T.H. was less on his surroundings but more on his health:

> *And now I come to the catastrophe of the trip. In jumping from the wagon which was in motion yesterday morning, I struck the edge of a dry wagon rut and my foot slipping, received so severe a sprain as to cause me to faint. My foot is still very badly swollen and I am for the present utterly disabled – unable to bear the slightest weight upon it. I hope however to get the use of it in a day or two.*
>
> *My health was never better. I sleep in the open air every night and suffer not the slightest inconveniences. I shall mail this at Julesburg.*

Even though T.H. evidently had the opportunity to become involved with a Denver newspaper, the following letter makes it plain that (at least at that time) he was not interested in the business:

> *2 Sept. 1861, from Denver City Book Store & News Room*
>
> *The "Rocky Mountain News" is struggling hard for an existence, and will, I fear, be forced into an assignment before many weeks – in all events, before the first of January. Your notorious husband has repeatedly been elicited to start a paper in Denver, with unexceptionable backing, but has not entertained the proposition for one moment.*

Many of the letters sent by T.H. during the fall of 1861 commented on the commercial prospects in Colorado and the enterprises that he and his father-in-law (Rich Hogeboom) were operating. And, T.H. complained frequently about the circumstances that kept him apart from his wife. Two that reflect these concerns are the following:

13 Sept. 1861, from Tarryall City [also called Buckskin Joe].

I left Denver Tuesday, and have been 4 days on the road, being detained by a sick horse. I hear from the mill that they are getting along pretty well sawing, but Sell little. I think I can improve the Sells

If your father fits out his trains with freight, notify me of the time they start. I will tell them at Buckskin that I intend leaving about the first of October; but it is possible that I may not get away before the 25th

25 Oct. 1861, from Buckskin Joe.

Why is it, Hattie, dear, that I can't get a line from you & I haven't heard a word, directly or indirectly, since I came up from Denver. If you are not ill, I know you would have written.

Indeed, it is probable that Hattie was feeling ill because she gave birth to their daughter Eva on November 6, 1861. (See more about this birth in Chapter Eight.)

The following summer (1862) T.H. and Rich Hogeboom swapped locations, that is, T.H. came home to Larimer and Rich went to Colorado. During that time, T.H. corresponded with Rich, partly about financial problems of the mill they owned jointly and partly about their business of equipping supply convoys between eastern Nebraska and central Colorado. T.H. may have also worked at odd jobs; for example, he once mentioned that he was stacking wheat.

In the fall the two men again swapped locations, with T. H. struggling again to make a living in the rapidly changing environment of the gold fields of the Colorado Territory. His letters to Hattie conveyed an increasing discouragement with his health, with his struggle to survive in the rugged physical environment, with the innumerable quarrels common in a frontier setting, with the uncertainty of making a profit by catering to the needs of miners, plus the financial risks of striking gold, What was most difficult, he ardently declared, was living apart from his wife. These adversaries are mentioned in the several of the letters sent during the spring of 1863 (which follow):

> *14 Jan'y, 1863, from Denver City*
>
> *I have nothing from you later than 9th December, but I suppose I have lots of letters at Montgomery. You don't know how I wish to see you! In my whole 7 months absence in 1861, I did not have so strong an anxiety to see, and be with my wife as I have for the last few weeks. In fact I think my affection for you is far stronger now than when we first exchanged vows at the altar. I suppose if I were making any thing here, I should not feel half so gloomy as I do now, but being away from home, and making no money at that, bears harder on me than ever before. I hope times will improve here before long.*
>
> *Now my love, take good care of yourself, and do not worry about too much. Remember how much depends on the ensuing two or three months* [because of the expected birth of another child].

> *21st Mar. 1863, from Denver City, C.T.*
>
> *I got back here* [from a place 50 miles away] *one week ago today; and I have been ill ever since. I got out yesterday for the first time – had the quinsy very badly, throat broke twice. Am now all right again, or shall be so soon, as I gain a little strength. I do not lose my courage, darling, but am stronger in the faith of ultimate success than ever. I think I can announce that*

we are through the cap in Montgomery; I have every assurance of it from persons up there. I am now only waiting for the teams to come down from Montgomery, to load them and send up which will be sometime next week. It will probably be about the first of June before we can realize anything from our Claim in Montgomery, besides paying up some debts.

Denver is exceedingly dull – the market overstocked with everything. A great panic exists among the bankers, and gold dust now is in small demand. I had assurance sometime since that, if I wished to go to Omaha about the 1st of April, that I could have $15,000 or $20,000 to take (for some bankers here) for which I should receive 1¼ per cent, or $12.50 per $1000. This would pay my expenses and more to go by coach, but unless a change occurs soon I shall have to abandon it because, at present, there is no likelihood of there being any dust to take in. Bankers are afraid to buy.

I have been offered, dear, a lucrative position ($200 per month and expenses) of a secret nature, such as I am not now at liberty to disclose, services to be rendered elsewhere than in this Territory, such as would keep me from home eight and nine months at least. The proposition is open until the 1st of May, which will give me ample time to determine whether our future is really made at Montgomery or not. Please say nothing of this, for although there is an apparent mystery connected with it, I can assure you there is nothing dishonorable. The seal of secrecy imposed is more because it is known to few and I may wish to avail myself of the offer. [N. B. T.H. never mentioned this "mysterious" offer again.]

3rd April, 1863, from Denver City
I have not heard a word from home and do not know now whether I am the father of a living child, the husband of a happy mother and fond wife, or whether the next

news I receive will bid me mourn for a life of a little one I have never seen, and possibly a contingency, which I dare not contemplate, the death of the only woman for whom I care, the only being on earth who cares for me. Am I to blame, if under these circumstances I feel sad, anxious, and even blue? I have this winter, Hattie, darling, prided myself a little on my nerve and courage under the most disheartening circumstances: I have made light of losses which I could ill afford, laughed at petty vexations and larger harassments, buoyed up as I was, by your sympathy, love, and I doubt not, your prayers. Illness I have not heeded, but now my soul is racked with the torture of suspense, such as I never before knew.

Dearest, you speak of our first little one, and I think I can appreciate your feelings at the reflection; oh, what would I not give to have seen her! [N. B. His apprehension about the upcoming childbirth was undoubtedly affected by the loss of their first child (Eva), who lived only 18 days.]

Borrow no trouble about my ever being forced into this war, it can never be prosecuted with an unwilling soldiery, and I do not believe that this [Lincoln] *administration, weak, imbecile, and wicked though it be, will ever be sufficiently foolhardy to try to enforce so infamous a measure. The war party, or rather the Abolitionists, called Democrats traitors and copperheads. Is it possible that they expect to make up an army of traitors? If they draft, they must take Democrats, or, as they call them, traitors. Bosch it don't alarm me a bit.*

22nd May, 1863, from Montgomery, C.T.
Between seeking "new diggings" (called in mining parlance "prospecting"), attending lawsuits before justices of the peace, striving to collect last year's debts,

endeavoring to price lumber sales wherever they are to be made, and reading and answering letters (mostly yours, my dear, which I peruse several times over), I manage to put in from 16 to 18 hours of time out of every 24 of the six days allotted for man's labor

I must say that I do want to see our boy. I suppose you will not object to my saying "our boy", even if he doesn't much resemble me. Very likely he doesn't differ much in personal appearance from other specimens of incipient manhood at his age; but then his partial paternal as well as idolizing maternal, would very properly, or at least naturally, invest him with powers and qualities of unusual precocity, and these helpless little fellows, whether precious, very pretty, or otherwise, have an unaccountable manner of worming themselves into very warm places of their parents' hearts. (I didn't intend the above sentence to suggest vermifuge.) I have no doubt that ours is, in all respects, a model baby, he must be. Do you give sufficient nourishment for him?

But anxious as I am to see the baby, I am still more desirous to see his mother; in fact Hattie, I am so anxious to see you and baby, that I can scarcely restrain the impulse to leave everything here, and hasten home; but reflection assures me that I am too old to indulge in such boyish freaks. So I consent to forego the pleasure of kissing my wife and child for a time longer. "The dear little episode"—as Artemas Ward [an American author] would say—I hope you kiss him often for his father.

For the next three months, T.H. was in quandary about what he should do. The high expectations that one of his two claims would strike gold followed by the disillusionment when they failed, the contradictory advice from his business partner (Rich Hogeboom) about future investments in Omaha and/or the uncertainty about the future of gold-rush towns of Colorado, plus various suggestions from his wife all created extensive doubt about what he should do and where. He even mulled over the pros and cons of moving to Montana or New Mexico.

In spite of his consideration of moving elsewhere, T.H. decided to return to Sarpy County in September 1863, where he remained the rest of his life. After returning home – and thus seldom having a reason to write to Hattie – the information about his activities is skimpy. He evidently continued working with Rich Hogeboom in their business of equipping supply wagons to the West and running a saw mill in Larimer.

One letter T.H. sent to Hattie during the final decade of his life (besides a few he sent to Hattie in the summer of 1865 when she and the children made a trip to visit relatives in the East) was from Lincoln when he was serving in the Nebraska Territorial Legislature:

9 Feb. 1866, from Hall of House of Representatives

I shall not likely come down home tomorrow, for the reasons that the Session will be late, and my health is too poor to stand a night ride. I was foolish enough yesterday to consent to preside over the House, with a large amount of business on the table to dispose of, and consequently much talking and reading to do. I am to-day so hoarse I can scarcely speak along, and my lungs are so sore that I am in constant pain.

The "Joint Resolution Submitting a Constitution to the people" passed the House yesterday by a vote of 22 to 16. We can brot [?] it before the people on the 2nd of June next.

I wish T.H. had kept a journal during the next several years, especially while he was serving in the Nebraska Legislature. But such was not to be. T.H. died in December of 1874. His obituary makes interesting reading, not only because it reviews his multifarious career but because the author's praise contrasts dramatically with the venom expressed by his political enemies during his newspaper years. The following was published in the *Omaha Herald* (Dec. 27, 1874):

> After an illness of about ten days Theodore H. Robertson died at La Platte of typhoid pneumonia, December 23, 1874, aged 50 years in March next. He was a native of Massachusetts, whence he removed to Ohio in his early childhood with his father, Gen. J. H. [sic] Robertson, who settled in the town of Amherst, Lorain County, where he [T.H.] was reared and educated. He read law, and was admitted to the Bar, in Elyria, and was subsequently married, removing to Nebraska with his family in the early part of the year 1856, at about which time his father Gen. Robertson was appointed agent of the Omahas. A poor memory of minor events may not enable us to recall the circumstances of Mr. Robertson's arrival here, but it is believed that he was at first engaged with Gen. Robertson in the management of the Omaha Indians. But soon afterwards [T.H.] succeeded John Sherman as the Editor of the *Omaha Nebraskian*, which was the first paper that was ever published in Omaha on a permanent basis, and continued his connection with that paper until a date which we do not now recall.
>
> It was not until Mr. Robertson became connected with the *Nebraskian* that it became a power in moulding [sic] the material and political interests of the Territory. He brought to it a vigorous mind, and an able, industrious and energetic pen. A Democrat from conviction he entered into the spirit of the cause he advocated with his whole soul, and fought for the men who represented it as though the fate of the nation and his own personal reputation and fortunes were bound up in the issue for which he was contending. He entered upon editorial life with a natural aptitude for a style of writing for which those times particularly called. If he did not always preserve what is called the dignity of the Press, he seldom failed to prove its power as a writer of clear and forceful English, and no man among us since that day had demonstrated more ability as a

journalist. It has always been a matter of regret with his friends that circumstances drew him away from a calling for which he was admirably fitted. He wielded a powerful pen, and it befell us to be frequently reminded in his later years that the diversions of widely different pursuits left its original strength unimpaired. Had Mr. Robertson continued in the editorial profession it is only just to his memory to say that he would have been the peer of the ablest and the best in the calling.

In the political strifes of the times in which he conducted the *Nebraskian*, he developed those qualities of self-reliance, fearlessness and independence, which, added to a rare fund of information upon which a ready memory enabled him to draw at will, made him a formidable adversary. Able and clear in argument, he was also a paragraphist of no mean power. If Mr. Robertson was not a close student, he was a careful and accurate observer of affairs, and few men were better informed of the political history of the country. He was a born politician, but he was more. A Democrat of unyielding convictions, he was a prudent counsellor in the affairs of that party which was always proud to acknowledge his leadership, as well in its later days of gloom and defeat, as in the brighter days of sunshine and victory. With what fidelity he adhered to the fortunes of his friend Bird B. Chapman when those fortunes, and those of his party, and ours, began to wane, all among us who participated in the scenes of those days will bear witness. But Mr. Robertson's memory would suffer a great injustice at our hands, if we failed to add to this sketch of his career as a political Editor the fact that, at the head of the *Nebraskian*, he demonstrated his ability to publish an excellent newspaper. That journal did much to invite emigration [sic] to this then unknown land by keeping before the people of the old States the salubrity of its climate, the beauties of its prairie scenery, and the exhaustless fertility of its soil. In the rivalries of those times between ambitious localities, he fought for Omaha with sustained zeal and the most determined energy. The delegation of representative citizens of this now large commercial city, who went to La Platte yesterday to pay respects to his memory, did not forget that they were to stand over the bier of a man who had done much to establish it upon its present broad and solid foundation.

Theodore H. Robertson was widely known and universally respected in Nebraska. He was not merely a man of strong intelligence. A great heart beat in his bosom, and to this fact he was largely indebted for the friendships that will long linger around his grave and memory. The fidelity of Mr. Robertson to friends was remarkable. He neither forgot nor deserted them. The greater the tests that were made upon his fidelity, the brighter did this quality shine in him. His political adversaries never failed to bear cheerful testimony to the natural generosity of his heart, and to the genuine goodness of his nature. These heart-qualities made him a kind, affectionate, and indulgent husband and father, and they shed their most genial influences around a fireside now so sadly bereft by the ruthless hand of the Destroyer.

Mr. Robertson was an active and influential citizen in private life. He served one term in the legislature of 1866, and was of course a leading member of that body. So far as we know, he never practiced his profession [as lawyer], but he owed much to the study of it.

Mr. Robertson was twice married, his first wife having died in Omaha, after a short and distressing illness, January 18, 1860. By her he had one daughter, the young lady whom we met yesterday among the chief mourners at his grave. He married Harriett [sic] Hogeboom, February 11, 1861, and leaves a wife and five children to mourn his loss.

The funeral of Mr. Robertson took place at his late residence at La Platte, at 12 o'clock yesterday, Rev. J. Paterson of this city officiating. It was largely attended by immediate friends and neighbors where he has so long resided. The feature that must have been peculiarly gratifying to his kindred was the large delegation of prominent ladies and gentlemen, who were present from this city and who thought they owed it to themselves and to his family and memory to pay this mark of respect to Mr. Robertson.

Long processions followed the remains to the grave. They repose in a beautiful spot on the high elevation overlooking the great valley of the Platte.

CHAPTER EIGHT

HARRIET HOGEBOOM

One of my great grandmothers on my Robertson/Wood side was Harriet (Hattie) Hogeboom. Hattie was born and died in Sarpy County, Nebraska, a fact that might suggest that she was not a part of the general migratory stream of my ancestors to Nebraska. However her letters indicate that she could have diverted a distributary of that stream to another state because she was an independent thinker who was ready to undertake new adventures.

Hattie's heritage, like that of most of my great grandparents, was primarily composed of several generations of persons born in America. In fact, an ancestor eight generations earlier (Joel Phelps) was a member of the American Revolutionary Army for a short time.

Hattie's surname comes from a Dutch ancestor (six generations earlier) by the name of Bartholemeus Hoogeboom. That family name does not match Hattie's surname because the spelling underwent modifications with subsequent descendants. In fact, sometimes the spelling of a particular person's name varied, even in a single message. Here I have spelled Hattie's and her father's name as "Hogeboom", even though her grandfather Dirk's surname was known as "Hogaboom".

Dirk Hogaboom was a prominent citizen of Sarpy County. He fought in the Civil War on the Union side, which is probably the reason for "Col." being affixed to his name. Col. Dirk Hogeboom was one of the founding "proprietors" of Larimer City (see sidebar on Larimer in Chapter 7) and he built the first hotel in that town. He worked with Dr. Erastus N. Upjohn in starting The Nebraska Palladium newspaper; and he was a Sarpy County Commissioner. He and his wife had 5 children, one of whom was Hattie's father Rich.

Rich Hogeboom married Phoebe Farnsworth (Figs. 28 and 29); they had four daughters, one of whom was Hattie.

Fig. 28 Richard Hogeboom, father of Harriet Hogeboom

Fig. 29 Phoebe (Farnsworth) Hogeboom, mother of Harriet Hogeboom

Harriet received some of her education at a convent in St. Joseph, Missouri. I do not know what her educational goal was, but a letter sent to her by her sister Cornelia, who was at home in Omaha (in June 1856) assured Hattie that "Father says he will send you the money to pay your music bill". A year later a friend who was still attending the St. Jo Convent wrote to Hattie (who at that time was living in "Omaha City, Nebraska Territory"); the friend included the phrase "when you get married". This remark seems to reflect the social life of her friend "Hat" (Hattie), who enjoyed attending cotillion parties (see Explanatory Panel "Cotillion Party").

Cotillion Party

Now and respectfully invited to attend

"COTILLION PARTY" to be given

at the Larimer Hotel at Larimer City on

Friday August 19th 1859

MANAGERS

Larimer City

* * *

Levi Kimball   Benjamin Bachelor

R. P. Rankin

* * * Plattsmouth

S. H. Jones   John Patterson

Joe Carpenter

* * *

Bellue

C. D. Keller   I. B. Kinzey

★ ★ ★

FLOOR MANAGER

S. A. Strickland

★ ★ ★

MUSIC

Pickin's String Band

Tickets $2.50

J. SAGHT, Proprietor

After graduating from the convent, Hattie taught school north of La Platte. It is believed that at the time of her graduation or when she commenced teaching, her father gave her the watch pictured in Fig. 30.

Fig. 30 Harriet Hogeboom's Gold Watch

The social events in the sparsely populated Larimer-Omaha region brought together persons with marriageable interests so it is not surprising that Hattie became acquainted with the widower T.H. The way their friendship intensified is unknown, but their relationship is verified by the following enthusiastic note Hattie sent to "Mr. Robertson" on the 2nd of November 1860:

> *Mr. Robertson,*
> *Your kind invitation is at hand & after a lengthy consultation of five minutes with that, I have concluded to accept it. I am of the opinion that my brains are in my heels. Come for me on Wednesday morning.*
> *Hastily & Respectfully, Hat A. Hogeboom.*

Hattie and T.H. married three months later (Feb. 11th, 1861). Hattie kept a diary for four months, commencing a week before their wedding and ending a week after they returned from a trip to visit relatives in Iowa and Ohio – and to bring Fannie to their home in Nebraska. In Hattie's diary entry for the 4th of Feb., (which I did not include here), she mentioned having a daguerreotype taken (Fig. 31).

Fig. 31. Harriet (Hogeboom) Robertson

Hattie and T.H. left immediately on their "honeymoon" trip. Hattie's perspective – and humor – are revealed by the following entries in the diary that she kept during the first half of 1861:

Sun. Feb. 10. Father brought my trunk & I packed it. Mr. R. came after dark.

Mon. Feb. 11. My wedding day. "A lowery day & a lowery Bride" an old old maxim. We'll see how mine is.

Tues. Feb. 12. Left Council Bluffs at 5 AM. Weather cold but bright & pleasant.

Wed. Feb. 13. Snowed in the afternoon. Got to Des Moines about 5 PM. Was pretty tired.

Thurs. Feb. 14. Storm still rages with unabated fury. Wonder how long we will be obliged to remain in this place.

Fri. Feb. 15. It has stopped snowing but is still cloudy. No stages to start today. Grant me patience, kind Heavens.

Mon.Feb.16. Started at 8 AM. Took supper at Grinnell. Traveled all night. I am tired of staging across Iowa.

Feb. 19. Windy, cold, rather unpleasant. Reach Ottumwa at midnight

Wed. Feb. 20. Went to Aunt Lib's; found them well; then to Grandpa's [Farnsworth] *in the afternoon. Back to Lib's & staid all night.*

Thurs. Feb. 28. Grandma's [Farnsworth] *to dinner. Took cars for Chicago at 2:20; got here at 6.*

Fri. Mar. 1. Bought me a summer hat. Leave for Ohio at 6 PM.

Sun. Mar. 24. The last day at Father Robertson.

Mon. Mar. 25. Left Amherst 10 min. past 7; reached Cleveland at 9.

Tues.Mar.26. Reached Chicago. Staid until 11 PM & took the train Changed cars at Galesburg this AM. Reached Quincy at 1 PM.

Thurs. Mar. 28. Crossed river, took train to Palmyra, then changed for St. Jo. Reached there at 10 PM, went right aboard the boat.

Fri. Mar. 29. Started at 2 AM on the steamboat Omaha. Wind is blowing strongly & is ahead.

Sat. Mar. 30. Still on the boat – tedious travelling. [N. B. Steamboat travel was not only "tedious" but it was also somewhat dangerous. An article in *Nebraska History* (1970) states that 295 wrecks occurred on the Missouri River from 1853 to 1897].

Sun. Mar. 31. Travelled all day; rather rainy. Most had the blues.

Mon. Apr. 1. Landed at Omaha; went to the Herndon. Had breakfast & went home to Larimer. Staid all night.

Tues. Apr. 2. Still home. Husband went to Omaha & left me here.

Thurs. Apr. 4. Sick all day with dyspepsia.

Sat. Apr. 6. Husband came for me, went back to Omaha.

Wed. Apr. 10. Staid in room all day. Made Fannie apron. Had a slight spat with R.

Even though this chapter concentrates on Hattie's life and what she wrote, it is interesting to read the dissimilar account of their "honeymoon" trip written by T.H. His comments about the same journey (see the following) display the adjustment these two independent-minded individuals must have experienced during their early days of marriage:

Jan. 10. Write to Hattie. Get teeth drawn.

Jan. 13. Ride down to Larimer with horse and cutter from Coffmans. See Hattie in evening. Stay all night.

Jan. 21. Ride up from Larimer in forenoon. Get my wedding cards.

Jan. 24. Get my copy in. At Maggie Mills party in evening. Load many presents.

Jan. 25. Get paper out in evening.

Feb. 11. Cold and blustering in morning; clear before noon. Married at one o'clock P.M. by Rev. Hamilton. Start for Council Bluffs, where we stop.

Feb. 12. Make 60 miles before dark in open sleigh. Hattie stands the journey very well.

Feb. 13. Rode all night, making 50 miles. Bad roads, deep snow, slow teams, and surly drivers. Breakfast at Adair at 11:30 A.M. Commence snowing. Reach Des Moines in snow storm.

Feb. 14. Weather bound at Des Moines House all day. Comfortable quarters. Hattie much refreshed after a good nights rest. Write back to Nebraskian.

Feb. 15. Snow very deep. No stages starting out. Still detained at Des Moines House, with prospect of several days' delay.

Feb. 18. Leave Des Moines at 9 A.M., weather cold. 12 passengers. Supper at Grinnell at 10:30 evening. Ride all night.

Feb. 19. Windy, cold, rather unpleasant. Reach Ottumwa at midnight.

Feb. 20. Visit Farnsworth, Hattie's grandparents in P.M.

Mar. 2. Took cars at 6:30 last night. Reach Oberlin at 8 this A.M. Get down to father's at 11 A.M.

Mar. 5. Call at Loretta's in morning. [T.H.'s sister Loretta married Parks Foster.] *At father Johnson's in P.M. Get old Abe's inaugural.* [N. B. Pres. Lincoln delivered it on Mon. Mar. 4, 1861]

Mar. 16. Go to Park's to dinner and to Elyria in P.M.

Mar. 24. Pack trunks. Take baggage down to Amherst.

Mar. 25. Leave Cleveland at 7:30 P.M. via Crestline for Chicago.

Mar. 26. Make slow time—detained by cattle trains off the track at Plymouth. Reach Chicago at 1:30 P.M.

Mar. 27. Left Chicago at 11 last night on Chicago B. & Q. R.R. At Quincy by 1 o'clock. Stay overnight.

Mar. 28. Leave Quincy at 8:30 A.M. Reach St. Jo 10 o'clock A.M. Take Steamer to Omaha.

Mar. 29. Leave St. Joseph at 6 o'clock A.M.

Mar. 30. Pass Brownville. Tie up at night.

Mar. 31. Pass Nebraska City in morning. Ride all night in boat.

Apr. 1. Reach Omaha at daylight. Go down to Hogebooms. Stay all night.

Apr. 25. Move into house on Dodge.

Apr. 26. Put down carpets.

Mon. June 10. Getting ready for Denver.

Wed. June 12. Start for Denver at 10:15 A.M.

The remainder of this chapter continues with the writings by and about Hattie. T.H. left for Colorado just six weeks after they returned from their honeymoon, which meant Hattie alone had to cope with financial matters and the care of Fannie. Those trials and troubles are described in the following letters:

21 July 1861. from Home Sarpy Co,

Yours from Denver reached me in due time, I was glad to hear you were well & in good spirits. My bodily health is good & I sincerely wish my mind was in as good condition. I am at present sitting with folded hands & a resigned look waiting for what will happen next; but perhaps I had better tell my story; then you will understand.

Last Wednesday afternoon I took Mrs. Cook home & staid with her that night. The next morning I went over to the house to see to my things. What was my surprise on entering to find the house stripped of furniture, even the beds & pillows were gone. I inquired of Mrs. Chapel & learned that Sutton had taken them two days before. I went up the street. I saw Sutton & asked what is meant? He said Lyman Richardson had a *note of $60 against you & had gone into court, testified that you were a non-resident of the Territory & that I had either gone to Denver or East. They managed some way to get the dining room window open, went in there & took the things out the back door. The tables, safe & stove are left. I told Sutton that Lyman had sworn to a deliberate lie & he should suffer for it. I then went to see Chapman; he was not in, so I stated the case to Sapp. He said the things were exempt by law from attachment, as you did not owe five hundred dollars' worth of real estate, which amount you were entitled to & that the attachment could be set aside without difficulty. I went home & sent Father up. He saw Chapman, who said it was all right, that he made a note of it at the time & told Sutton he should sue him.*

Just imagine, if you can, how happy I must have felt trotting through the streets on boiling hot day hunting up lawyers, marshals, sheriffs, etc. I wished for the while that I had never seen your face. Why in the name of sense did you not tell me you owed Lyman & what is it for? Had I known of it, I might have spared myself the humiliation of having my furniture taken by a sheriff. Great scalding tears of mortification & wounded pride streamed from my eyes even as I write, spite my effort to keep them back. I kept my courage up while I was in town in order that the people might not know that I cared. I guess Father will begin to think that in taking you for a son-in-law, instead of getting rid of me, he has one more to do for & take care of. Now then I want you by return mail to make a candid statement of just how your affairs stand in Omaha. Who you owe & how much. How much Clark owes you. What security you have & everything else about it. I have not asked you before because you have always said, a man should make his wife his confident in business as well as other matters, & I supposed you did, but find I stepped wide of the mark.

If I have any more trouble I am going to let the furniture go. I would sooner live on a crust & eat it off the floor than feel as though I owed any man. If you think I am severe just place yourself in my shoes for a moment, a five months' wife & already have had two affairs of the kind to settle for my husband. You know how galling it must be to a person of my disposition. I fear we committed a mistake.

I shall write you how the affairs terminate.

Their correspondence during the next couple months seldom mentioned financial matters. Hattie's letters usually contained news about her activities and comments that revealed a growing relationship of love.

10 Aug. 1861, from "Home"

Yours of the 27ᵗʰ came safely to hand. I suppose by this time you have the mill running. Father says to sell as soon as you can possibly, for he wants to get rid of it. You know well as he what would be reasonable.

I almost wish you would take the paper back again. [N. B. Here again is a reference to the fluctuating feelings that she and T.H. had about his association with a newspaper.]

I wish I could send you some corn & potatoes. If you will take dinner with us, you may have all you wish. I live on corn & cucumbers.

My dear husband, I've nothing more to say, so I'll stop. I might fill another sheet, telling how much I miss you & with expression of affection, but it would only give me the blues & you too, so I'll not.

24 Aug. 1861, from Home Sarpy Co.

Father thinks you had better sell the mill & take stock if you can do no better. He is making arrangements to raise stock. He thinks you will make well selling lumber at $40 if you find ready sale.

16 Nov. 1861, from Larimer City

To Mr. Robertson from Cornelia Hogeboom [Hatties sister]

My dear Mr. Robertson

I've written one letter to you directed to Hamilton, and now will write and direct this to Denver. I've but a moment to write so I'll come at once to the main object of this letter, viz the moment of your daughter's arrival. She made her debut on the 6th, rather earlier than she was expected. Hat is doing well so is the baby. They are with us. Hat came down to spend the day and was taken sick immediately. She employs Upjohn.

Haven't another moment to write. Excuse brevity.

Yours affectionately Cornelia Hogeboom

Baby weighs three pounds! Better stay at home and help Hat next time.

The birth that Cornelia (Nellie) reported was that of Eva, who lived only 18 days.

During the summer of 1862 T.H. was home, which meant there were no letters telling about the lives of Hattie and T.H.. for several months. Later that year after T.H. returned to Colorado, which created the need for a continuation of their correspondence. Some of Hattie's letters lacked sufficient background information for one to understand exactly where she was living and what she was doing to earn money. Nevertheless, many of her writings discussed the pros and cons of their being away from each other, and a few included a consideration about her moving to Colorado. The following letters cover the remaining time T.H. was away:

5 Dec. 1862, from "Home"

4 days of pleasant sunshiny weather have passed since you started for the land of gold. During that time I have had so much to occupy my mind – moving & settling – that I have not had very much time to miss you.

I cannot tell how much I hated to have you go. More, if possible, than I did last year. I moved down Monday. Am now quite comfortably fixed. I think the sitting room, the pleasantest one in the County:

Since you left we have had no Nebraskian.

16 Dec. 1862, from "Home"

We are all getting along like "Pigs in clover". I have had any amount of customers. The "Plattsmouth Company" stopped with us one night – had lodging to the amount of $6.00;116 meals & feed for horses, making over $50.00. O. P. Mason & Capt. Bedford staid all night last Thursday & the Monday before the Bishop [a small stern-wheel steamer] *put-up with us. Little Buck Board Billy's father is here & wants to rent a house this winter to burn lime & work the land in the Spring.*

Father asked me this morning if you wouldn't be likely to stay at Montgomery all Summer. I told him you said "Maybe you would stay two years". He (father) still talks of going out to the mountains this winter. He asked Mother if it would be much work to make two or three hundred pounds of sausage to take out.

I hope you will take excellent care of yourself, & remember, I am coming to see you in the spring. No preventing Providence. Cornelia says she shall go too. I shall not remain a widow two years. You will want to see your family before that time. Won't you?

11ᵗʰ Jan. 1863., from "Home"

My health is pretty good, also Fannie's. The weather still continues splendid. I almost hate to stay in this house, and I presume if it were not for my goodly proportions I should be as all over creation. Aren't you glad there is something to keep me at home?

Cornelia had a letter from one of her Farm Ridge friends. They were sorry you were obliged to leave me but so glad you had not gone back to the paper; it almost reconciled them to having you stay four years instead of two, as I told them. I can plainly see father does not intend you to come back right off. He laughs at the idea of my going out there, but I'll show him & you too, if the Lord spares my life & health. Your Mother thinks the best thing you can do will be to send Fannie & I there, but I differ with her somewhat.

14th Jan. 1863., from "Home"

I am glad & sorry to hear you are a little homesick – glad as it goes to show that you do care for your troublesome wife, yet sorry because I think you ought not to come home. Father, I am sure, does not want to spend another summer there – he said so. And I do not think you would live through another summer on the farm. You know I shall be well taken care of & I have every confidence that I shall have a good time. Then, about June, if you are able to bear the expense & I the journey, I will come to you. I am willing to make any sacrifice to get along now, while we are young & healthy. If you do well, as I am confident you will, we need not be separated for long. So cheer up & pitch into business with a good will & a determination to succeed at all hazards.

Fannie is well & a very good girl. She reads a good deal. When I get some money, I shall get her a Mental Arithmetic & Primary Geography. She reads Bible histories & understands them better than many an older person.

Mrs. A. L. King has a big boy weighing 12 lbs. Mine will be about that size. I am a sight-to-behold.

7 Feb. 1863

Your welcome favor of the 24ᵗʰ January came to hand last night. I was very glad to hear you were well; but am sorry the Blue devils still have the ascendancy; remember the song you used to sing so much:"Stare fate in the face". [N. B. This was the theme of the popular song "Trust to Luck".] *I have every confidence in your ability & know you will succeed in making a living, which is all we want. It is worse than folly to spend the best part of one's life striving to lay up treasures on earth. We can take none of it with us & we cannot live long enough to enjoy it. "Do with your might whatever your hands find to do." Keep a cool head & clear conscience and I promise you will be more than content.*

I shall not insist on going to the mountains, but if I am able to take such a trip with children & you feel able to bear the expenses, I should enjoy it. I want you to stay there till the business is all closed up & you need not go back. I guess we will both be able to stand the separation. Absence will make the heart grow fonder & we can settle down & spend the remainder of our days in a never waning honeymoon.

My health has been better for a week than since you went away. I am very pendent. I stay at home very close. Aunt Mary worries for fear I do not take exercises enough; but I follow Upjohn's advice, not hers.

16 Feb. 1863

I want to do everything that is reasonable & right, but still I beg of you do not for a moment indulge in the idea of moving Fannie & I to the mountains for I cannot consent to it. I want to go next summer if the trip will not involve too much expense but shall not unless

I can return in the fall. I am not able to work hard & should be more expense to you there, than here. And as long as your family is here, there is a prospect of your coming back some time. I had sooner be here & poor than be separated from Father & Mother for an indefinite period.

They are both old & getting feeble. Now don't get out of patience & call me unreasonable, for I can not help it. My whole soul gets up in rebellion at the idea of living in the mountains. I am not afraid of a Northern rebellion, neither is any one here. You know I am more fearful of Indians than anything else.

22 Mar. 1863

I thought I should not write you again until some time in April but I am sure you will be glad of a few lines. My health is tolerably good. The rest of the family are as usual. I begin to get tired waiting, have hardly been out the house for two months & it is so pleasant now. You can not imagine how badly I want a horseback ride.

I still want to go see you next summer but shall not stay with you. Will bring you back with me if I can. Worry some about your health. You must put yourself under a physician's care. Our folks will write you as soon as your child arrives.

Now take good care of yourself for the sake of your family & loving wife. Write often & at great length; forget all about politics.

3rd Apr. 1863, from Larimer City
My dear Mr. Robertson,

Hat desires me to write you a line this evening, appraising you of the arrival of Richard – your son & heir – the arrival this morning at ten o'clock. He is a

*tolerably fine specimen of a boy – weighing upwards of
ten lbs. Hat is doing well*

*Excuse brevity – I have bad eyes and the lamp light
hurts them.*

Cornelia Hogeboom

27 May 1863, from "Home"

*Your family are all well, especially your boy, who
grows very fast & is, I think, quite a noble specimen of
humanity. The baby has not red hair. Everyone but me
thinks he resembles you. Beck Bennet says "Why he
looks more like Mr. Robertson than Mr. R. does like
himself." His eyes are a very deep blue.*

*I am sorry your prospects are still dull, but very
much pleased to hear you keep up your spirits so well. I
should not be sorry to hear you had the new gold fever.
I have some confidence in those mines.*

2nd July 1863

*The country generally, has been thrown into a great
state of excitement over this wonderful battle which
Capt. Edwards fought with the Sioux & in which Dyson
lost his life.* [N. B. She is probably talking about the
June 23rd confrontation when Capt. Edwards attempted
to deter the Sioux raid against the Pawnee Reservation.
He received a slight wound in doing so.]

*Your boy grows finely & is getting very interesting
to his Mother; he laughs & plays a good deal. Fannie
is well. I do not think Cornelia will marry right away.*

30 Aug. 1863

*I will begin with the concluding & most important
remarks in your last. I hope you will not think of going
into a paper in Denver or any place else; I never shall
consent to go there & live. Father says he hopes you*

will come home before you make any arrangements out there. He thinks you can do better here, raising stock.

I suppose you will hear before this reaches you of the execution of Judge Cyrus Tater. He died protesting his innocence, but no one believed it. [N. B. The first legal execution in Nebraska was Cyrus Tater in Aug. 1863.]

10th Sept. 1863

I suppose I shall see you soon now. Then there will no longer be any need of this provoking mode of talking.

Indeed, their correspondence did mostly end after T.H. returned home. A brief exception occurred when Hattie, Fannie, and Baby Dick visited relatives in Ohio during the summer of 1865. Hattie's letters follow:

29 May 1865

Grandpa's folks are about as usual. Grand Ma walked down to church yesterday. I went to Church & heard a man eulogized as a "Saint" [Hattie followed that with a question mark.] *who was assassinated in a theatre. Mr. Crook has a large picture of Booth! He is a very handsome man.*

I will write again as soon as I reach Ohio. Give my love to all the folks. Fannie sends love. She wants to go back to Nebraska very bad.

15 June 1865

This morning my revered father-in-law let me drive his favorite Gypsy down to the Corners. Sarah paid my fine horsemanship the compliment of riding with me. Your father never lets even Frank or John drive his horse, so you see I am in high favor.

What are your prospects for going into a paper this fall?

11 Sept. [1865]

Last Monday night I went with Mr. Cunningham and wife to a commencement concert – it was splendid. Miss Lizzie Gates of Elyria was principal soprano. The concert was conducted by Prof. Morgan's oldest son who had just returned from Germany where he has been completing his musical education.

No messages from Hattie followed this September one, which indicates the family returned home as planned. Probably T.H., Hattie, and their children were not apart for more than a few days the rest of her life. Without letters or diaries, I do not know the personal events for the last decade of Hattie's life, but she must have been busy with a growing family.

Fannie married Edward J. Upjohn, the son of Dr. Erasmus N. Upjohn, who was an early settler of Larimer and Sarpy County (mentioned above). After Dr. Upjohn died, his widow (Mary) married Rich Hogeboom in 1888, thus connecting the Robertson and Hogeboom families doubly.

Richard (Dick) Robertson – the next living child – is not discussed here because he is the focus of Chapter 11.

In 1866, Elizabeth (Elsie) Lorain Robertson was born. She always went by the name Elsie, but her close friends nicknamed her "Dimple". She was certainly more independent than most females of that era. She engaged in a variety of ventures, ranging from traveling to writing obituaries, poems, and essays (Fig. 32). She also assumed the role of family genealogist (although she sometimes embellished the achievements of ancestors).

Fig. 32. Elsie Robertson at her typewriter

The next child was John Henry, who lived much of his life away from Nebraska (including what he regarded as a few "glorious years" in the Army during the Spanish-American War). He and wife Cora visited Nebraska fairly regularly in later years and they welcomed visits to their California home from other members of the Robertson family

The last child of Hattie and T.H. Robertson was Bertha Harriet (born July 1873). She married William Vogel; and they, with their two daughters remained in Omaha the rest of their lives. (Their son moved elsewhere in later years.)

Hattie did not live to enjoy the adult lives of her children. She died in March 1875, less than three months after her husband's death. Her demise meant their four children (Fannie age 20, Dick 12, Elsie 9, John 6, and Bertha 2) became orphans.

I end this chapter with an obituary of Harriet (published in the *Omaha Daily Herald* on March 9, 1875).

Sad News From La Platte –
Death of Mrs. T. H. Robertson

Mrs. Robertson, wife of the late Theodore H. Robertson, died at La Platte Sunday night after an illness of about ten days.

We much regret the loss of this lady, and the calamity to her suddenly orphaned children. The cause of it would not be difficult to trace to the grief and cares that came upon Mrs. Robertson with the death of her husband. She follows him to rest and peace. Our sympathies are not for her. They gather round four young fatherless and motherless children, who are left painfully bereft by the visitation of "sudden death". We hope God will direct their tender care and protection, now and hereafter.

Mrs. Robertson has been long known to many as the daughter of Mr. Hogeboom, near whom she resides. We knew her long and well. She was a most intelligent and estimable woman, and was widely esteemed in all her relations of life.

In order to give the friends of the family in Omaha an opportunity to attend it, the funeral will take place on Thursday next at La Platte. Rev. Reuben Gaylord, of this city, will officiate. We trust that there will be a large attendance of our people on the melancholy occasion.

CHAPTER NINE

LEVI WOOD

Levi Wood was one of my four great grandfathers (the others being Amos, Benton, and T.H.). I know he did live in eastern Nebraska a brief time; but much of Levi's life is obscure. I am guessing this absence is because he was a person who did not write much.

Another handicap in learning about Levi's life is the commonality of names. This was apparent one time when Sally and I were searching records in Cooper County, Missouri. We were excited when we found a notice in an historical library listing an abandoned cemetery called "Woods Family Cemetery No. 1" near Prairie Home (a small town in Cooper County). We noted its location and promptly drove to the home of the farmer who owned the land. He took me to an overgrown plot in the center of a field. After pulling weeds from the tumbled down tombstones, I excitedly examined two broken tombstones: one for "A Wood" and the other with the name "Levi Wood". My initial exhilaration soon dissipated when I realized the birth and death dates on the headstones did not even come close of those of my ancestors. I had to conclude that the graveyard was linked to an entirely different Wood family.

As I searched documents stored in libraries and courthouses, I was able to piece together several basic bits of information. However, this kind of source was incomplete because a fire destroyed the 1780 census records in Tennessee, where Levi's parents (Alexander and

Nancy Wood) lived earlier. Nevertheless, I was able to piece together some of his biographical information.

Levi M. Wood was born (February 1829) in Cooper County, Missouri, where his father (Alexander Wood) owned land. It is not known why Alexander and his wife Nancy moved from Tennessee to central Missouri. It may have been the lure of new land in a region where ownership of slaves was also allowed. Alexander was a slave-holder. This fact was documented later by the 1860 Slave Census for Cooper County, which reported that Alexander owned eleven slaves and his new wife had two.

Levi was working on a farm at the time the 1850 U.S. Census for Cooper County was taken. However, it seems that within two years he had moved to Gentry County in northwest Missouri.

Why did Levi move from central Missouri to the northwestern part of the state? I have no information that might reveal a motivation for his move; but I assume his occupation was farming and he could acquire more land by migrating westward at this time.

During the next eleven years, Levi married Eliza Ann Gentry; and they became the parents of six children (see Chapter Ten for details of their offspring.)

In July 1863 Levi moved to Nebraska, specifically to Sarpy County. Even though Levi did not leave any written materials that would explain his motives for moving, events in the region suggest a strong justification for leaving his farm in southwest Missouri. The turmoil that was occurring in Kansas and western Missouri undoubtedly created a hostile environment – one that would motive a man to see refuge for his family (see Explanatory Panel "Political Conflicts of the Civil War Period. At that time, Sarpy County was relatively safe from the chaos farther south. It was a newly developing region that was not too far away.

Political Conflicts of the Civil War Period

In 1854 the U.S. Congress passed the Kansas-Nebraska Act of 1854, which changed the rules about slavery. Rather than enduring Congressional battles involved with balancing the admission of pro-slavery and anti-slavery states, the new Act declared that future states would henceforth decide this issue. It specified through the vote of white male settlers currently residing in each Territory (that was requesting statehood) would decide whether it would become pro-slavery or anti-slavery. One of the immediate effects was a time of lawlessness in Kansas, which spilled over into nearby Missouri.

The region suffered from the militant bands of Jayhawkers (free-state supporters) and Border Ruffians (pro-slavery advocates).The raids by both of these bands of men who robbed, fought, and killed for their beliefs or, in many cases, just for revenge, plunder, or land, finally led to a declaration of martial law in Kansas and western Missouri in February 1862.

The details of the life of Levi, as well as his family, during the decade they were living in Nebraska is unknown. Based on scattered comments (which appear in subsequent chapters), I deduce that the family participated in the Sarpy community activities. And, I assume Levi continued farming. During their time in Nebraska, Levi and Eliza Ann had two more children. The accompanying picture of Levi (Fig. 33) is not dated but I am assuming this is a fair depiction of his appearance at this stage in his life.

Fig. 33 Levi Wood

In 1872 Levi and family returned to northwest Missouri, presumably to his former farm. By this time the older two sons were nineteen and seventeen years old and left the family nest.

Eight years later (in Oct. 1880), Levi died. (His body was buried in a cemetery in Worth, which is a portion of the former Gentry County).

Soon Eliza Ann and the girls returned Sarpy County, Nebraska. Several of her activities and of her girls are described in the next chapter.

CHAPTER TEN

ELIZA ANN GENTRY

Eliza Ann Gentry was my great grandmother, that is, she was my mother's grandmother. Eliza Ann migrated westward in a series of moves that ultimately ended in Nebraska. Most of her locational changes seem to have been related to the decisions of her father or her husband – except her final one to Sarpy County.

Several generations of Eliza Ann's forefathers lived in North America. They included her paternal grandfather's great grandfather, who came to the Colony of Virginia in the 1680s; and her maternal grandfather, who served in the Revolutionary War. The homes of other forebears were mostly in Virginia, New York, and Kentucky.

It was in Kentucky where Martin Gentry, Eliza Ann's father, first lived, married, and became the father of four children. After his first wife died, Martin moved with his children to Putnam County, Indiana. There Martin and his second wife (Jane Cornell) became the parents of six children, one of whom was Eliza Ann (born Dec. 1830).

Two years later, Martin and family resettled in Gentry County, which is located in northwest Missouri. [N. B. The county was named for a colonel in the Seminole Wars – not for any of Eliza Ann's relatives.] It is believed Martin acquired land there and engaged in farming.

Several years later Martin left home and headed for the gold fields of California – a decision that greatly changed the lives of his family. I do not know why Martin Gentry decided to leave his farm and family to go west; probably it was the fame of the California Gold Rush of 1849 that enticed him. His long range goals are not clear. He may have considered moving permanently to this perceived "land of opportunity". On the other hand, his second letter (see below) indicates that he decided it should be only a temporary move. In any case, in the spring of 1850 Martin headed for California to dig for gold. Following are the two letters (saved by his descendants), in which he described his journey and some of his experiences and feelings.

29 May 1850, from Grand Island, to Jackson Gentry
I will just rite a few lines to let you no that wee are well but myself. I have been somewhat porley for a few days but getting better again. The balance are well and spry as a Buck, but have not caut nare Squaw yet. Our cattle all stands the trip so far first rate.

I will give you some acount of the Country wee have traveled threw. It is one of the prettist country that I ever saw and the best rode that I ever saw so fare. It is one of the gratest for farming that is in the world provided it was rightly proportioned with timber. It is perfectly dry and just roling a nough for farming.

29 September 1850, from "Goald digins Callifornia", to Andrew Gentry
I will rite you a few lines to let you all no that wee all got thru alive that is more than I expect thousands done without a very long and tedious trip. As for my part, I had very bad health the most of the way but not so bad but what I could walk the most of the time I landed threw where wee have stoped verry much reduced and verry weeke but I am gaining slowly and in hope to get well once more

George and BreckRidge is well and harty and george bout out a little grocery and is attending to it

*and brack has bin mining some but has not made much
out yet I have not bin to look round yet but from what
I can here among the people there is but few that is
making enny thing a mining. there has bin some that
has bin lucky to hit a good lead and have made money
very fast. it is like lottery some get a great deal with
the work and some others may work a great deal and
get little. I understand that there is a great manny that
went out this spring is aleaving and going home wee
have stops in a new place fifty miles on this side of
Sacramento Citty those was a few that has stoped when
we got in and now there is fifty houses, I expect tho I
have not counted them, and a great many wagons. Some
in that has not commenced bilding yet and still coming
in every day. it beats all countrys that I ever saw for
little provision stores groceries. There is fifteene or
twenty now and I expect there will bee not les than fifty
here this winter. There is too beef markets here and tha
have the best beef I never saw in enny country and sels
at 20 and 25 cents per pound & 18 cts potatoes + 20
cts a pound onions one dollar per pound Chees 1 dollar
pickle pork 35 cts There is a great deal of hauling from
the Citty by horse,*

*Now i will say some thing a bout our journey wee
left the missouri on the 14 of may past fort Carney 29
fort Larremy on the 14 of June and then wee past over
the Backbone of the world on the first day of july and on
that morning there was ice in our water bucket wee got
in sight of the snowy mountains about the 25 of june and
then on snow every day untill the 7 of august except the
30 day of july then it took us untill the 17 of September
before we got in to the great goald digging*

*A few words about our wagon and team wee never
broke the first thing about our wagon or team and got
them all thru except whiteback, she giv out in the forty
miles & went and then wee left her little slower stood*

the second best of enny thing that was in the team jack stood it the best the wagon never turned round but what he was in the town and he was the only one.

Now a word or too to enny body that wants to come here next spring let him stay at home enny body that has a family and enny way to maintain them let him stay at home and them that has money one half of them wood do better at home; a word to dads man Simpson my advise is to stay with your lake the balance of your life and the same advice to Andrew Wood.

Now as for the sickness on the way i expect you have heard more than i am able to rite to you; it has bin very bad, now am better; conserning my self i have money enough to take me threw the winter if i dont get season work and then i shall have to stay untill i can make enuf to come home on

Wee will relocate on what is called dry diggns and . . . [The remainder of the letter is unclear.]

Unfortunately Martin's endeavors ended a couple years later when he died somewhere "near Sacramento" (possibly Coloma, California). I have no information about the circumstances of his death or about the disposal of his body.

After the death of Martin, his widow (Jane Cornell) was left with several of their younger children, including Eliza Ann. I have no information about her early years. After reaching adulthood, Eliza Ann married Levi Wood (in 1852). They eventually had eight children. Here I include only the six who are mentioned in subsequent chapters: Frank, Archey, Laura, Alice, Della, and Clara.

As explained in the previous chapter, Levi and Eliza Ann moved with their family to Larimer, Sarpy County (Nebraska) in 1863. While the family was there, Della and Clara were born. It was probably while in Larimer that the following two pictures taken (see Fig. 34 and Fig. 35).

Fig. 34 Eliza Ann (Gentry) Wood   Fig. 35 Eliza Ann with
                                     Della and Clara Wood

After Levi's death (Oct. 1880), Eliza Ann made a major decision: she returned to Sarpy County with her youngest daughters. It is difficult to deduce her motives for that move, but apparently she remembered being an active member of a Sarpy County community (after Levi and family had fled from their Missouri home). She must have wanted to spend the rest of her life in Nebraska.

Eliza Ann lived in Sarpy County for a decade, during which time she celebrated the marriage of her daughter Della Jane. Eliza Ann died here a few days before her 70th birthday.

When I read the obituary copied here, I was surprised by the amount of detail that described the circumstances of her death.

In Memoriam

Died. At her home in LaPlatte, Monday, December 2, at 1 o'clock a.m., Mrs. Eliza A. Wood, aged 69 years, 11 months and ten days.

Mrs. Eliza Wood, whose maiden name was Gentry, was born at Greencastle, Ind., December 23, 1830, and while a child was removed with her family to Northern

Missouri, being among the first settlers in that section of the state, in fact Gentry County was named for her father. [N. B. This was not the source for the county name; see above.] She was married to Levi Wood, February 5, 1852. During the year of '63 they came to Nebraska, and were numbered among the oldest settlers of this country. After a period of nine years, they returned to Missouri, where Mr. Wood died October 5, 1880. Three years later Mrs. Wood returned with her family to Nebraska and has been a resident of this county ever since.

During the past year she suffered such constant and acute pain from sciatic rheumatism and neuralgia, as to completely shatter her nervous system, and to some degree unhinge her mind. Shortly after noon, on Saturday, she got a two-ounce bottle of laudanum [see Explanatory Panel] from the safe in her room, and drank the contents.

Laudanum

Laudanum, also known as Tincture of Opium, was an alcoholic herbal preparation containing about 10% powdered opium. Until the early 1900s, laudanum was sold without a prescription and was a constituent of many patent medicines. In fact, cocaine, heroin, cannabis, and other similar drugs were sold legally in the United States prior to the Pure Food and Drug Act of 1906.

Her son-in-law Mr. Louis [sic] Iske saw the act, too late to prevent it. She could not realize the fatal consequences of her act, and although strong emetics were instantly administered, nothing availed, as her stomach was completely empty at the time, and therefore the drug penetrated her system at once, and sent her into a deadly stupor from which nothing could arouse her. Dr. Kelley, of South Omaha, used every means to arrest the progress of the poison, but all was futile. Congestion of the brain ensued, and death resulted at 1 o'clock in the morning of Monday.

Funeral services were held the afternoon of the same day, Rev. Wm. Nichol, of Bellevue, officiating, and Tuesday morning the remains of Mrs. Wood were taken to Worth County, Missouri, for burial beside her husband. So ends the earth-life and work of one who bore away burdens and heavy sorrow with Christian patience and fortitude. She has laid down her weary cross of sorrow and suffering to enter into rest. Who shall question the Infinite Wisdom that saw fit to call her, in this way, through the gates of life? The God she loved and trusted may perform His mercies in a way mysterious to us, but it is His hand, and we know His will is best.

Five children are left to mourn her love – Mr. F. Wood, Mrs. Levi Long, Mrs. Lucien Reed, and Mrs. R. H. Robertson, of this county, and Archibald Wood who resides in Missouri.

To the memory of the deceased the following verses are lovingly dedicated: [N. B. Only half are copied here.]

The "following verses" were authored by "E.R.", which undoubtedly refers to Elsie Robertson. I have included only half of her verses, but the remaining ones convey Elsie's "loving dedication".

> Let no rain of bitter weeping fall
> For her whose pain has ended.
> Though we miss her at the hearthstone,
>   Where her empty chair is set,
> She had heard loved voices
> Calling from the Land beyond the River,
> And her heart longed for the dear ones
>   Waiting on the other shore.
> Through the shadows, darkly falling,
> She has passed from earth forever,
> To a land that has no partings

And where sorrow comes no more.
Let the tired hands stay folded;
Let the dim eyes close forever
In this world, to open gladly
In a brighter world above,E. R.

CHAPTER ELEVEN

RICHARD H. ROBERTSON

Richard Hogeboom Robertson, my maternal grandfather, who was born in Sarpy County, Nebraska, seemed to have a great desire to live elsewhere. Although he moved to several other locations, numerous unpredicted circumstances resulted in his repetitious returning to the place of his birth.

Richard Robertson, who was usually called Dick, was one of the first Euro-Americans born in Sarpy County (on 3 April 1863). By the time Dick was twelve years old, he was an orphan: his father (T.H.) had died in December of 1874 and his mother (Hattie) had died the following March. Immediately after Hattie's death, Dick's paternal grandparents in Ohio assumed responsibility for him and his younger siblings. However, Dick soon returned to Nebraska, but the other youngsters remained in Ohio until they were older.

Dick's step-sister, Fannie, who was 20 years old at that time of Hattie's death, was also invited to come to Ohio to live with her mother's relatives, as is revealed by the following letter written by Sarah, the sister of T.H.:

18 Apr. 1875, from S. [Sarah] M. Robertson, North Amherst

My dear Fannie

I can hardly call to mind when I last wrote to you, or you to me. On my part it is not that I have forgotten you, neither that I do not feel a deep interest & sympathy for you. When we heard the sad tidings of your mother's death, I thought I must write to you at once. We have all felt most deeply for all of the poor orphaned ones out in Nebraska. Of course we know that as you are so much older than the others, you must, of course, feel the great loss very keenly. Of course you are most tenderly attached to your brothers & sisters, & not only have to mourn on your own account, but that the more helpless children are bereaved.

Your Uncle Andrew has seemed to feel tenderly anxious about you. He has a very pleasant wife & three children. Before he heard of your mother's death, he wanted me to write to see if she was willing that you should come to Ohio. I promised him to do so. After your mother's death he seemed to feel more anxious to hear from you but his children have been sick with Scarlatina [scarlet fever] *& he wanted me to write for him this proposal to you. If you would like to come out here, that he would send you money & bear your traveling expenses & would give you as good a home as he has for himself & family. Then after a sensible time if you were not content here, he would see that you had the means to go back to Nebraska.*

I think you remember enough about your mother's family here to be able to judge for yourself, about the kind of surroundings you would have. Andrew seems to think of you tenderly as his sister's child. I think he would do all that in his opinion would be necessary to promote your happiness. I have written just what he told me to, & not knowing very much of your present

*circumstances do not feel at liberty to advise. I think I
am not mistaken in thinking that you have been trained
to act conscientiously & have so much confidence
in Mrs. Hogeboom & Mrs. Luce that I think they are
better prepared to give you advice than I can. One
thing I do wish you would do, & that is write to me very
confidentially for I do feel a deep interest in your future.
Grandma joins me in this request.*

Yours affectionately, S. M. Robertson.

Fannie declined that offer, stayed in Laramie, and a few years
later married Ed Upjohn. Fannie and Ed remained in Sarpy County
for several years and maintained a close relationship with Dick (see
correspondence below). Dick's younger siblings also returned to their
birth area after they reached adulthood (see Chapter 8)

Tidbits in family records suggest that Dick's Aunt Nellie (Cornelia
Hogeboom; see Fig. 36) and his Hogaboom grandparents gave him
personal assistance during his early teenage years in Sarpy County.

Fig. 36 Cornelia (Nellie) Hogeboom Luce

Evidently he found a variety of odd jobs to earn his way.

When Dick was 18, he joined a crew surveying for the Union Pacific Railroad. His diary of that time (which he titled "R.H. Robertson, Fort Omaha, Nebr. 1881" and subtitled "Of our trip up the Muddy, commencing Sept. 4th 1881; J.E. Sherlock, Asst. Engineer, U.P. Ry. 1881-82") gives insight into his work as a rod man, his health, and his aspirations for his future. The following selected entries from his diary are interspersed here chronologically with portions of letters sent to Fannie (which are marked "Diary" or "Letter").

> *April 10th 1881, from Estes Park, Colo.* [Letter]
> *Dear Fannie.*
>
> *Aunt Nellie told me in her letter that you were unwell. I hope you have recovered and are feeling as well as I am to night. I have never felt better in my life than I do now. This kind of work agrees with me perfectly, and I like it better than any jobs I ever tried before.*
>
> *We are now about 32 miles from Loveland and have closed our survey up the Big Thompson, and are now going down the Boulder to survey a line up the Boulder Creek.*
>
> *Last Sunday was my 18th birthday and I could not help thinking how differently I was situated, and felt, than one year ago that day.*
>
> *Wednesday Sept. 7th* [Diary]
> *Traveled up the Muddy all day, and camped at night at the foot of Whitney Peak. We saw a great many antelope today. This evening Mr. Smart and myself went hunting. We wounded four antelope, but they all got away.*
>
> *Sunday, Oct. 16th.* [Diary]
> *I wrote to Aunt N. a letter today announcing my intention to stay with the party until it goes in.*

Sunday, Oct. 30th, 1881, In Camp on Blacktail Creek
[Letter]
Dear Fannie,

I am to be promoted two steps at one time, day after tomorrow, the 1st Nov. It will be a little harder work but I will get $10 per month more for it. I will be rod man, that is the highest rank in the party, except the rank of men who use the instruments. The prospects of my getting "the rod" was the only thing that induced me to stay as long as I have.

Write soon to your brother, R. H. Robertson–600 miles from home and 40 miles from nowhere.

Sunday Nov.20 [Diary]
I am feeling very weak. I managed to walk six miles from Cozzen and then I played out. I paid a man a dollar to let me ride on up to the summit, six miles. Our team reached here to night.

Tuesday Nov. 22d [Diary]
I received a check for my October money today. Got it and my other checks cashed. Am feeling better. It seems that our work is not over yet.

Wed. Nov. 23d [Diary]
Boarded the cars for Denver which place we reached about 8 P.M. They put 8 of us in the European Hotel but the rest of the boys are put in the Wentworth.

Saturday Dec. 10th [Diary]
Still in Denver but I expect to leave this evening. Mr. Sherlock is going to send me ahead with our outfit; the rest of the boys follow tomorrow. Where we are going however we can't find out.

Monday Dec. 12th [Diary]
Still on the road and getting very tiresome it is too. I am so sick & can't sit up half the time.

Thursday Dec. 15th [Diary]
The doctor came to see me this morning before I was up. He thinks I am better. Mr. Sherlock and some of the boys came in this evening.

Saturday Dec. 17th [Diary]
Feel about as I did yesterday: the doctor says I'm doing well I don't know whether I can stand the monotony of this much longer or not. When Mr. Stinson returns I shall make a strong endeavor to get to go home until after Christmas. The doctor says I will not be fit for duty before that time.

Wednesday Dec. 21st [Diary]
Am feeling pretty well though very weak. Mr. Stinson has got in; we decided not to send for Aunt Nellie as I am getting along all right and the trip would only put her out. Mr. Stinson has promised to get me transportation home as soon as I get strong enough.

Sunday Dec. 25th Christmas. [Diary]
Well Christmas is here and here I am 200 miles from home flat on my back. I am afraid it is going to be the most gloomy Christmas for me in a good many years. I can't help thinking of home somehow and the good time they are having there. I hope some of them are thinking of me. I feel pretty well today, and the doctor promised to let me get up, but he was here a while ago and told me I had better keep quiet: so there is no help for me and I will have to lie here all day though sorely against my will. They are getting up a pretty good dinner today but I will have to take mine in bed, as usual – confound

the luck. I have just received word from Aunt Nellie expressing sympathy for me. Oh dear I wish I could start for home right away but I can't.

Monday Dec. 26th [Diary]
Feel better this morning, am getting stronger right along. Mr. Stinson came in to see me this morning and he paid me $45 my wages for this month. He left town this afternoon, for camp. He will stay with the boys till Mr. Sherlock comes, which I expect will be in a day or two. I shall talk with him when he comes and ask his advice with regard to studying engineering. What I want to do is to stay with the party a few more months as rod man, and learn to run the rod. That I think will help me.

Thursday Dec. 29th [Diary]
I am going home just as soon as the doctor will allow it. After I recover my health I shall commence study, and shall apply myself diligently to my work. I have fully made up my mind to be a civil engineer.

Saturday Dec. 31st 1881. [Diary]
Well I am feeling stronger today than I have felt for over two weeks. The doctor was here this morning and I paid him his money: $27 for which he gave me a receipt. He thinks I can start for home tomorrow, says I will have to be very careful of myself this winter and advises me not to go out again into the field before spring. I do not think I care to lay in camp this winter for $15 per month.

Well the year is about done, a few more hours and it will be a thing of the past. It has been rather an eventful year for me. I have seen a good deal of Colorado, learned a few lessons in human nature. Seen a good deal in regard to surveying, and have been paid for it all instead of having to pay for it. What I have seen of surveying and what I have seen and heard of the men who are, and who call themselves surveyors and engineers has caused me to make up my mind to become not a surveyor but a civil engineer. I feel confident that I can accomplish it and I will.

January 1ˢᵗ 1882 [Diary]
Commenced the New Year with a ride to the depot (to see about my things) and a walk back. I feel first rate, and I guess I can start for home in good shape. I am going on the 7:42 P.M. express.

Dick spent the next couple months in the Omaha area, where he visited Fannie and Ed Upjohn and other relatives. Evidently he recovered enough from his illness that he was able to rejoin the surveying crew, this time in an area south of Pocatello, Idaho. He then continued his diary and letters to Fannie, as follows:

March 18ᵗʰ Pocatello [Diary]
Arrived here this morning. The town consists of a section house, and two or three cabooses, in one of which there is a telegraph office.

Monday April 3ʳᵈ 1882. [Diary]
Is it possible that this is my 19ᵗʰ birthday? It does not seem like it, but still it is true. I wish it was untrue. I should like to be a schoolboy of ten years of age once more. I am of the opinion that our happiest days are our school days. I know that I was happiest before my twelfth year than I have been since [my mother died].

Sunday, April 9ᵗʰ, from Coreys Camp, Oregon Short Line [Letter]
Dear Fannie,
    I hope Ed is getting better, I hope he is still better and feeling as well today as I am. I have been perfectly

well and getting better ever since I landed in Idaho, I feel natural once more, now that I am out "on line" four or five days in a week. I like the country first-rate, but I don't like the work as well as I did the work I was on last summer. It is not so very bad yet, but I am afraid it will get awful monotonous along about the 4th of July. I am rodman for Mr. H. Rohwer, an engineer architect formerly of Omaha.

Tuesday April 11th [Diary]
Storming. Stayed in camp all day. Studied algebra.

Tuesday May 24 [Diary]
Rec'd a letter from my grandfather [Hogeboom] the other day. He wishes me to send him all the money I can spare and he "will try to squander it for me". I shall send it to him as fast as I get it. I have no way to invest it out here and if I draw it out here I am liable to spend it foolishly. I think I shall go back there in September anyway, probably and go to school in the fall and winter; I have wasted time enough.

Aug. 10th 1882, from Camp on Dempsey Creek [Letter]
Dear Fannie,
Your letter surprised me in due time. You deserve a chromo for your promptness. [N. B. A chromo was a colored print made by lithography. This may have been when the picture (shown as Fig. 37) was taken.]

Fig. 37 Richard (Dick) Robertson

Ed, how is that bronco of mine getting on. I don't
suppose you have sold it yet for $250 have you.

Information about Dick for the next several years is available from letters to Fannie. An exception to that source is his obituary, which stated that he went "to Omaha where he attended a school a short time, educating himself to be a civil engineer". In his letters to Fannie Dick reported that that he was doing custom baling in Dodge County. For example, in August of 1895 he reported that "after we got the press repaired, we went out at 10:30 and pressed all night until 6 A.M. and pressed 130 bales". In addition, he mentioned a couple interests not related to work. One was the entry which amusingly stated that "the 'nine' went over to Hershey where they played a ball game against the Blacklegs but lost 45 to 15." The other (written the last day of November of 1885) states that he attended "a poetical lecture".

Dick's life entered a new phase in October 1889 when he married. He first met Della Jane Wood when she and his sister sang a duet one evening, an event that soon led to marriage (see Fig. 38, which I assume was taken about this time).

Fig. 38 Della and Dick Robertson

Dick and Della had three children. The first child, Richie, was born in May of 1892; but he died three years later. The second child, Dean, was born on May Day, a few days after his brother's death. The third child, Nainie, was born the 19th of November of 1895 (see Fig. 39).

Fig. 39 Dean, Dick, Nainie, and Della Robertson

During the last decade of the 19th century, Dick was busy with several jobs: he did land surveying, operated a general store, and served as postmaster in La Platte. However, for some unknown reason, Dick and Della gave up their store and headed for the West in the summer of 1901. Why? Was it because they believed Dick's health would be improved in a different climate? Maybe so, but yet whenever he became quite ill, the family returned to the La Platte-Omaha area. Probably the motivation was a yearning for land in a different part of the country. The rest of his life seemed to display a tension between two geographical attractions: one was the location of his birth place and the other was some distant region where, he believed, held more promise. Initially his geographic goal was southwest Idaho or southeast Washington. Later he considered getting land in Oregon, western Washington, Wyoming, Minnesota, and Texas.

Dick did not continue a diary after 1885, but many details about his work, aspirations, and family moves are contained in Della's diary. Therefore, I have used her diary comments as a reliable source about Dick during later years of his life.

Della wrote that, after selling their store and home in La Platte, they headed west on July 8, 1901. In August of that year, Dick and Della bought a 6.1-acre fruit farm near Clarkston, Washington. However, because of Dick's "poor health", they reluctantly sold that farm in December 1905. They moved to southern California in hopes that he would regain his health there.

Unfortunately Dick continued to have more medical problems while in California, so they returned to Nebraska in March of 1906. In August of 1907 they bought a one-acre farm south of South Omaha. To supplement the family income, Dick did some surveying and served as rural mail carrier. Two years later (Aug. 15, 1909), he left for Bullard, Texas, to "look for land"; but "the climate was unsatisfactory for him". In Sept. 1916 the family looked for land near Bruno, Minnesota, but "did not find anything suitable".

In the spring of 1920 Dick resigned from carrying rural mail from South Omaha "because of poor health". Evidently he believed that he had recovered so on May 19, 1920, Dick and Della sold their South Omaha acreage and headed west. Ten days later they arrived in Deaver, Wyoming, where son Dean was "working for the government". After a few days, Dick, Della, and Nainie continued westward. In late July the three of them arrived in Nampa, Idaho, where they bought a house and looked at land around Fruitland, Idaho. Apparently they were unsuccessful because in mid-August they journeyed to Ontario, Oregon, "to look for land". They did not find anything satisfactory, so Dick worked for several weeks as a day laborer picking apples.

It was at this time that it was hypothesized by family, friends, and/or doctor that Dick's poor health was caused by infected teeth. Therefore, on Feb. 23, 1921, Dick had all his teeth pulled. Later the family became convinced that the massive extraction did not lessen his medical problems, but instead, the procedure had worsened his health.

Dick must have improved somewhat and returned home. However, Della noted on May 16, 1921, that Dean took his father to Portland, Oregon, for medical treatment. It seems that again Dick recovered enough that in August he and Della moved to a 6½-acre fruit farm near Newberg, Oregon. They were unable to buy it, but Dick worked as day laborer briefly. Two weeks later they gave-up and returned to Omaha. They stayed with relatives for several weeks, with hopes of finding a house of their own.

Dick's next – and final – move was to a hospital in Lincoln. The remaining days of his life were described by Della in the following three entries in her diary:

> *Dec. 12, 1921. We took Dick before the insanity board; he was adjudged insane and taken to the State hospital for treatment. John R. and Dean went with the sheriff to take Dick to Lincoln in an Auto.*

> *Mar. 30, 1922. I was down to see Dick today. He is very low. The Dr. says there is no hope of his recovery,*

the flu left him so weak. He seemed clearer in his mind than usual, and talked more; seemed interested in things at home. I felt when I said good-by I would never see him alive again. He realized his condition and asked how long he could hold out. He is just a shadow of his former self. I would feel more reconciled if he was at home so we could make his last days as easy as possible.

April 1, 1922. We got the sad news of Dick's death this morning. Dean was at the depot to take the train to go to see him. We got word in time to stop him from going. Brewer – the undertaker of So. O.– will look after the body. We feel so sad and lonely, to think he had to die out there away from home and loved ones. We made the funeral plans; we will hold the services in Bellevue church Monday Apr 3rd, Dick's 59th birthday. Burial will be at La Platte where his relatives are laid to rest. Nainie was at home for the spring vacation from Peru, when we got the sad news.

Occupationally Dick was a surveyor, both public and private (Fig. 40); but he was happiest when he owned a horticultural farm.

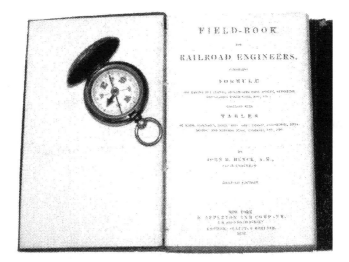

Fig. 40 Surveying Equipment of Dick Robertson

However, circumstances often necessitated doing other jobs such as being a farm hand, serving as postmaster, carrying rural mail, and selling goods.

Although the obituary of Dick summarized the major events of his life, I believe it missed the essence of the man because it does not consider his horticultural aspirations and the numerous adjustments forced on him by poor health. The following obituary appeared in the *Papillion Times* on April 6, 1922)

R. H. Robertson Passes Away.

Richard H. Robertson, one of the first born in Sarpy County, died last Saturday after an illness of over a year. He had been in failing health the past several years and a few years ago went to Idaho in hopes that a change of climate might be helpful but he steadily grew worse and he was unable to rally.

Born April 3, 1863, in La Platte in this county, he was left an orphan twelve years of age and had to make his own way in life, early coming to do a man's work. He spent his youthful years at the home of his grandfather, later going to Omaha where he attended school a short time, educating himself to be a civil engineer.

On October 2, 1889, he was married to Miss Della Wood, which union was blessed with three children. Richie, who died at the age of three years, and Dean and Nainie, both of whom are still at home. His widow also survives, and one brother, John H. Robertson and two sisters, Miss Nellie [sic: it should read "Elsie"] Robertson and Mrs. J. W. Vogel, all of Omaha.

Mr. Robertson spent practically his entire life in the county of his birth. He served two terms as county surveyor, and from 1911 until 1920 was rural carrier on Route No.5, out of South Omaha. His health failing then he resigned and went to Nampa, Idaho, where his illness came upon him from which he was unable to rally.

The funeral services were held Monday afternoon at 2:30 at the Bellevue Presbyterian church. Dr. R. L. Wheeler of South Omaha, officiating. Burial was in La Platte cemetery where on the top of a commanding hill overlooking the place of his birth and the scene of so many years of his labors his mortal remains were laid tenderly to rest. The pall bearers were J. M. Gates, S. W. Gramlich, John Covin, G. C. Reed, John Frazeur, and Clarence Way, all men who grew in manhood with him in the same community.

CHAPTER TWELVE

DELLA WOOD

Della Jane Wood was a person who demonstrated a continual vacillation between the attraction of distant places and the magnetism of a home place. It seems that most people have an internal struggle between the desire to experience new lands and the attachment to a particular place. Admittedly there are exceptions: individuals, who suffer from agoraphobia may have no desire to leave home while hobos may choose to always be traveling. My ancestors exemplify such differences in their migratory behaviors, although not to extremes. It seems that particularly Della had to confront the equipoise between these two pulls.

Della (the name she normally used) was born on the 5th of December 1867 in a cabin in Sarpy County, Nebraska, where Levi and Eliza Ann Wood lived for a few years. Later Levi took the family back to northwest Missouri (where they had lived previously); but after his death, Eliza Ann, moved her youngest daughters back to Larimer, Sarpy County. Della remained there during her youth (Fig. 41).

Fig. 41 Della Wood

A glimpse into Della's life prior to marriage is afforded by her autograph book. There are entries by John Robertson (Dick's brother) and Dimple Robertson (Dick's sister), which suggest they felt a special relationship to Della even before she became Dick's bride. The autographed entry by Dick himself (December 1888) was properly addressed to "Friend Della" and closed with a formal "Very truly yours". This may not be surprising, though, because Della couched her request to friends in a rather reserved manner:

To My Friends,
My album is a garden spot
Where all my friends may sow
Where thorns and thistles flourish not
But flowers alone may grow
With smiles for sunshine, tears for showers
I'll water, watch and guard these flowers.

In October 1889 Della married Dick Robertson. The circumstances of their meeting were described in a letter their daughter Nainie wrote to her fiancé years later:

> *My father first saw, and was attracted to my mother at an entertainment when my mother and his sister sang a duet. He liked music and so enjoyed the love song and the plump, sweet-faced singers. Later they met, and as La Platte was a tiny place, a stranger was always considered quite an event. He was a smart, efficient man and mother liked him. But it was several months, perhaps, before they became partners at affairs. I think it wasn't too long – several months – before he proposed. Then, after the engagement, he was gone some, but he wanted her to accept other escorts and go, and not be lonely. She had proposals within a few months – in all, she had four or five.*
>
> *Oh yes! you will be surprised to learn that grandma (mother's mother) took a dislike at first to father since father was an orphan at the age of twelve. This hurt mother, because grandma welcomed mother's sisters' beaux and husbands, and they weren't near the man my father was. But father went over to see Mrs. Wood and asked her what her objections were. She could name none, and began to like father then and kept on.*
>
> *Mother and father were very happy together and had few misunderstandings. When he was tired & impatient (for nerves made him so, often) she forgot it and kept sweet. When he saw she was tired and hurried and out-of-sorts, he was sweet and nice. So they learned to live and to let live.*
>
> *Father's father* [T.H. Robertson] *was a lover of books and a worker but he was a poor business man. His wife* [Hattie] *was a very capable person, much younger than he. She was a second wife and was early left a widow with four young children and little money.*

In six months, at the age of 36, she followed her husband to the "Land of no Return". She probably died of worry & broken-heartedness.

Mother's father [Levi Wood] *was a very patient, religious, overworked man, and filled a grave at the age of 52. No doubt doctors could have prolonged his life had he lived in the twentieth century. Her mother* [Eliza Ann Wood] *lived to the age of 72, and was a fine woman, but over-worked and kept in ill-health by having and raising a large family.*

Della and Dick's first child Richie (Richard Theodore) was born in May of 1892, but he died of diphtheria shortly before his third birthday. An obituary (undoubtedly written by Elsie Robertson) follows:

You have left us, little Richie. You have passed into the Silence, and another ring is forged, another link added to the golden chain which binds us to heaven. We have heard the ripple of the dark river rising above the restless surge of the tide of Life, and through blinding tears we have laid you to rest with the loved ones gone before.

We who tread the thorny ways of life will now mourn that your baby feet wearied thus early on the pilgrimage and stepped aside from our path into the sunshine eternal. The radiance of the celestial country enfolds you, and even we who are left desolate may catch faint glimpses of the glory into which you have passed. Only a little while and we shall find you again – those little hands so lately filled with apple blossoms, outstretched to welcome us to the fields of asphodel. [N. B. In the English poetic tradition, the meadows of the afterlife were covered with asphodel flowers.]

The second child of Della and Dick (Dean Leroy), was born on the 1st of May, 1894, a few days after Richie was buried. A year and a half later a close knit family of four emerged when their third child,

Nainie, was born. In later years, Nainie stated that she was born in a room behind a general store and post office. She remembered that "my mother took charge when father was away surveying." Undoubtedly Della was busy with household tasks and the care of two young children, as well as doing Dick's work when he was away from home.

Della's life was changed abruptly on the 8th of July 1901 when (as reported in Chapter 11) the family "said good bye to La Platte". They boarded a train and headed westward. For portions of their trip, they were accompanied by relatives and at several stops they visited other friends and relatives.

When they reached Wenatchee, Washington, they "saw some nice fruit farms that raised fine apricots, peaches, apples, and small fruits of all kinds". They continued to Seattle, then to Spokane, and finally to Moscow, Idaho. There Della and the children stayed at a hotel while Dick explored to find a fruit farm. On the 3rd of August (1901) Dick returned to Moscow with the news that he had found a suitable farm for sale. By the 12th of the month Dick and Della had decided to buy that fruit farm of 6.1 acres, which was located near Clarkston, Washington. They made arrangements to occupy the land the next day by pitching a tent. On the morning of August 14th 1901, the family immediately began work. Della wrote: "We pitched our tent, I got dinner, and we went blackberry picking".

Many years later, Nainie expanded on this same situation by writing the following:

> *I remember living in a one-room shack and sleeping in a tent. When father went away to do surveying, a neighbor girl came to stay with us. My mother kept a revolver under her pillow, but the only time she shot it was when she killed a rat. My mother worked so hard on the small farm she developed "a nervous stomach" and could not eat all the various fruits we produced. Dad was often surveying, irrigating the farm, or working as*

secretary for the Fruit Growers Assoc., through which we sold our fruit.

In mid-September, Della reported being very busy canning various fruits. She said that Dick was spending some of his time getting their house built, especially because it was "very rainy and disagreeable sleeping in the tent". Finally on the 30th of October the family moved "our beds upstairs in the new house".

Della was always very involved with the work of the fruit farm. They picked and canned more than 100 quarts of berries that season. Della and Dick worried about the occasional adverse weather, especially frost, and they were anxious about prices for their produce.

Della and the family also enjoyed the good side of life. They all enjoyed visits by friends and relatives from Nebraska. Nainie wrote later (see Chapter 13) about her fond memories of living on the farm near Clarkston. All four of them must have enjoyed seeing the Lewis and Clark Centennial Exposition in Seattle in August of 1905.

Della did not explain in her diary why they sold their Clarkston acreage but probably they had to abandon operating their horticultural holding because of Dick was again experiencing very poor health. It is not clear whether they could have retained ownership while renting the enterprise to someone else. Della explained the situation by writing: "We were ready to go to Calif. on Sat. the 25th (of Nov. 1905), but sold our home here and will have to postpone our going for a while. We rec'd $4450 for 6.1 acres."

In December the family did move to southern California, probably in hopes that the climate might help Dick recuperate. Nainie later noted that the time in Long Beach, CA., was "a terrible strain for poor mother who hardly slept at night and who spent every day at the hospital". Della wrote that "Dick is very sick from nervous collapse and was taken to the California Hospital in Los Angeles." A couple weeks later Della admitted that: "I have had a week of the worst mental strain of my life. I have spent every day at the Hospital and have gotten but little sleep at night. Mrs. McDonald spent two nights with me and the children." On the 2nd of March Della stated: "Dick is just out of the hospital; we expect to start for Omaha tomorrow."

After four days' train travel, Della and family arrived in South Omaha; they stayed with friends and relatives in La Platte and South Omaha until November (1906). They lived in rental housing for nine months, then they bought a six-room house with an acre of land planted to fruit in the South Omaha area. Della expressed her pleasure by writing: "It seems nice to have a home of our own once more."

Things went along fairly normally for several years: Della raised chickens, the two children were in good schools, and Dick had a variety of jobs such as surveying and carrying mail.

It was at this time that world events greatly impacted the life of Dean and the other members of the Robertson family. Therefore, even though Dean was not a direct-line ancestor of mine, I am interrupting my narrative about Della to describe the life of my Uncle Dean.

Dean's school years were in Clarkston, Washington, and South Omaha. He went to college briefly, but soon had to quit because of eye problems. While taking a Freshman Rhetoric class (January 1914), he wrote a poem expressing his desire to farm, which included the lines: "there is one place you always feel life's worth the while – that place? – in many tongues the reply is The Farm."

Dean's passion for farming was not realized immediately. He went to Montana for work in Aug. 1914, but returned home after a month. He then worked at Swift's for four months before going to Worland, Wyoming; however after five months he came home for a catarrhal operation. Next (in March of 1916) he was employed by Marshall Bros. Nursery in Arlington, NE. A year later he moved to Gretna, Nebr., bought a team and wagon, and began what seemed to be a realization of his occupational goal: to farm.

Dean's occupational goal was not to be. On the 6th of April 1917, the majority in the U.S. Congress declared war and the country became involved in World War One. By Thanksgiving Day 1917 Dean began selling his crops and livestock so he could enlist. Although he initially was drafted, subsequent circumstances led to his enlistment in the Marine Corps in January of 1918.

From Dean's letters and diary, the family has a fairly complete record of his experiences in the military. [N. B. Many of his papers are now with the National World War I Museum in Liberty, Missouri.] The most memorable event for Dean was a battle in France during which all but nine in his platoon of 43 men were killed. His survival affected his outlook and personal perspective the rest of his long life.

After the war, Dean tried to find land in various parts of the country. For example, he attempted to acquire some in Wyoming by government lottery, but did not "win" such. He still had not found a farm before he married Charlotte Boge (November 1923). He then felt the need to earn money immediately so he took a job in Lincoln, Nebraska, with the Chicago, Burlington, & Quincy Railroad. Although later he purchased a small acreage on the outskirts of Lincoln, his main income for the remainder of his life was derived from manual and supervisory labor in the rail yards.

Now, as the discussion returns to the life of Della, it chronologically overlaps previous comments about Dean. In late 1916 Della and Dick bought a thirty-acre farm south of Gretna, Nebraska (for $128.50 per acre). Three years later they sold their Gretna acreage and, along with Nainie, again left Nebraska for their dream fruit farm. Della's comments about this decision sound somewhat less enthusiastic than when they had previously migrated westward: "We sold all furniture except two stoves. We are footloose – no home." On their way, they spent a few days with Dean in Deaver, Wyoming, where he was "working for the government". Della, Dick, and Nainie arrived in Nampa, Idaho, in late July.

The following years were filled with many frustrations as Della and Dick pursued their dream of horticultural land and work, but being thwarted by Dick's reoccurring poor health (see more details in Chapter 11). This tension persisted for more than two decades following their decision to leave Sarpy County in July of 1901.

Della became a widow in the spring of 1922. Shortly afterwards she and Nainie moved from Omaha to live with Dean. The following diary entries by Della described the events that formed a close family unit that affected each of their lives:

> *May 22 1922. I rec'd life insurance $2000 from M.W.A. and $3000 from Western Life. We [Della, Dean, and Nainie] want to buy a home as soon as we can find one suitable. We are very lonely without our loved one. Home will never be the same again.*

> *Aug. 28 1922. We looked at an improved acreage near Lincoln; it is 15 acres belonging to Rothermal. We offered $8000; he took us up. We put $100 in the Citizens Natnl Bank of University Place to bind the bargain til the abstract is brot to date.*

> *Oct. 26th 1922. We moved today [from Omaha] to 50th & Vine St. Lincoln. Weather ideal. Mr. Schrins of Bellevue moved our goods in a truck for $30. Dean and I came in the Ford loaded down. We will get the cow & calf later. This is a very pretty place.*

Della became busy with raising chickens, gardening, and occasionally traveling, usually with Dean (who received train passes from his railroad employer). Often Dean attended conventions of the VFW [Veterans of Foreign Wars] while Della enjoyed seeing famous places.

> *June 8, 1923. The last of the chicks came off June 6th. I have only about 325 all told. I had poor hatches and bad luck raising them. I sold early chicks May 28th for only 30 cts. per lb. This has been a busy spring: put out 1050 strawberry, 300 asparagus, 300 grape vines.*

Sep 17 1924. I just returned from a trip to Washington D.C. Dean and I left home the 12ᵗʰ and spent the 13ᵗʰ in Chicago. That night I left for the East and he left the next day for St. Paul to attend the American Legion convention. I visited Walter Reed Hospital, Mt Vernon, Arlington Cemetery, Congressional Library, the White House, Capitol Museum, and other places of interest.

Della was also busy visiting family and community organizations. The following reports some of those activities, as well as some of her views on world events.

Nov. 29, 1924. This is Dean's wedding day. He married Charlotte Boge at Glenwood, Iowa. Nainie and I were with them.

Thursday, Oct. 1ˢᵗ, 1925. Dean and Charlotte are the proud parents of a daughter – Mary Virginia.

Apr. 18, 1926. I returned from Auburn today after spending a few days with Edna and Otto Kiel and the Stoddard family.

June 22 1926. This is the date I became a member of the order of Eastern Star lodge at University Place Nebr. I enjoyed the ceremony and glad to be a member of such an uplifting organization.

July 23ʳᵈ 1926. Nainie and I returned today from ten days in Colo. Springs

Sun. Aug 21 1927. This is Nainie's wedding day. She and Hugh Stoddard were married at noon today [in the Robertson house] *by Rev. A. K. Williams. They left for their new home near Brock Nebr., 60 miles away, where they have their home all ready, on a farm. Nainie's dress was blue silk and georgette; she looked so well.*

Nov. 7 1928. Hoover won over Smith. Six million votes, for which we are all thankful. Smith is Wet and a catholic, and a member of Tammany.

Jan [n.d.] 1933. Conditions all over the world are the worst I have ever known. Millions of men are out of work. Farmers are losing their homes. No price for crops or stock. There is no way to raise funds for taxes or interest on mortgages. Also homes in the city are being lost, as men have no jobs and can't make payments on their homes. Foreign countries are even worse off. Where will it all end?

Oct. 8 1933 Dean and I returned from Chicago. We spent two days at the World's fair, Century of Progress. The exhibits were fine. Big crowds. Our expense was only $4 apiece. We got nice rooms at the N.R.A. [National Rifle Association] *Hotel for $1 apiece, three blocks from fair grounds.*

After Della lamented (in January) about the terrible economic conditions, it seems surprising that in October, she took a pleasure trip to the 1933 World's Fair. I suppose Della justified her indulgence during a time of adversity as most people do because most people cannot constantly endure calamity.

Feb. 14 1935 I am starting for Los Angeles at 6^{10} P.M. on the C.B & Q. [to visit brother John and his wife Cora.]

July 13 1936 Dean and family & I myself leave tonite for Washington D.C.

I believe Della quite enjoyed her life in the 1930s (see Fig. 42) because she was physically able to be busily engaged in so many activities, as well as being intimately involved with close family members.

Fig. 42 Della (Wood) Robertson

By 1938, however, her diary entries were filled more with medical problems. In April of 1938 she was complaining of neuritis in her back, and in December of that year she reported that a doctor had drained 1½ quarts of water from her abdomen. The following year she wrote that an X-ray showed a growth on her liver. In February 1941 Della noted that a quart and a half of water was being drained from her abdomen almost weekly, and her enlarged liver was crowding "the digestive organs and other organs". She lamented that breathing was becoming difficult; and she was unhappy that a doctor had warned her that she had "a heart problem".

Della's afflictions increased after being bitten by a rat in December 1941. She described the incident as follow: "I had the misfortune last night to be bitten by a rat on my left little finger. He was in a basket of apples and got caught in the corner – I got too close to him." Within a few months she was taking both diathermy (a high-frequency electric current that generates deep heating) and X-ray treatments routinely. By December of 1942, the doctor was treating considerable infection in her left arm.

Della's diary ends on December 10th (1942). Her final days are described in Nainie's diary:

> *Jan. 1 1943 We drove to Lincoln to help cheer mother who is suffering from osteomyelitis of the left elbow.* [N. B. Osteomyelitis (OM) is an infection of the bone or bone marrow. Signs of OM include fever, pain, and swelling in the area of infection. It may result from an injury to the bone or from animal bites.] *She is bed-ridden and seems so weak. She has sort of lost her fight.*

> *Jan. 12. Mother went to Bryan Hospital where Dr. Weidman is preparing her for an operation on her elbow.*

> *Jan. 13. The doctor opened her left elbow and removed a piece of bone as large as a walnut. The Dr. thinks she would not have lived without the operation.*

> *June 1. I went to take care of Mother. She has a fever; and she is very discouraged.*

> *Sept. 30 Mother has felt fine for a month. She was so happy to feel herself.*

> *Oct. 7. Mother passed away at 8 P.M.*

The following obituary for Della was published on page 1 in the October 14th issue of the *Gretna Breeze*:

Mrs. R. H. Robertson, LaPlatte Pioneer, Died Oct. 7

Mrs. R. H. Robertson, a long time resident of LaPlatte and vicinity, died October 7 at the home of her son, Dean L. Robertson, in Lincoln. Her husband, who died 21 years ago, formerly operated a store in LaPlatte and served as county surveyor of Sarpy County.

During the Civil war Levi Wood with his wife, Eliza and children moved by ox team from the border state of Missouri to the comparative quiet and safety of Sarpy county, Nebraska.

In a cabin a few miles west of what is now Fort Crook, Della Jane Wood was born on December 5, 1867. She died at Lincoln, Nebr. at the home of her son on October 7, 1943, having attained the age of nearly seventy-six years.

While she was still a small child, the Wood family moved back to Missouri and it was there that Della grew to young womanhood. Life on the frontier was not easy and it was there that Della developed the habits of thrift and industry which characterized her entire life.

She then returned to Nebraska and has spent almost all of the years since in the vicinity of her birthplace or at Lincoln.

She taught school for a time and was united in marriage to Richard H. Robertson October 2, 1889. To this union three children were born.

She was a long time member and an active worker in the Methodist church and its various organizations together with the W.C.T.U. She was also a member of Myrtle Chapter No. 94, Order of the Eastern Star.

Her church, her home and her family were her chief interests.

Burial was in LaPlatte cemetery the ground for which was donated by Richard Robertson's grandfather.

CHAPTER THIRTEEN

NAINIE ROBERTSON & HUGH STODDARD

In previous chapters, I related stories about the migrations of my great grandparents and grandparents who left various places in northeastern United States and eventually arrived in eastern Nebraska. The result of those movements was that both my parents were born in this state. That, in turn, increased the possibility that they might meet, marry, and have children in this same locale. They did, in fact, meet while attending college. Eventually they married, and this chapter reveals factors that led to their marital life at Sunny Slope Farm.

My father, Hugh P. Stoddard, was born at Sunny Slope Farm (Nemaha County). He never strayed far from his birth place – although he was away for his higher education and a brief teaching job. The following is a description of what he titled a "Biographical Brief":

> *Having been taught at home, I was put in the third grade my first year in school at Clifton. The next year the three in that class were advanced to the sixth grade. However, as an eighth grader, after taking the county examinations, it was decided that I should spend another year in Clifton. I did not expect to go to high school, as our family considered many of the high school*

subjects of no value to a farmer. [N. B. This attitude about the superior status of a farmer seems to reflect the dogma of Hugh's grandfather Benton. Nevertheless, Nella (Benton's daughter and Hugh's mother) sent all her children to the School of Agriculture and encouraged post-secondary education.]

Later I sensed I was being left out socially. I could not talk with others my age about things they were interested in. Mother thought the atmosphere in Brock school was not wholesome. Lois and Wayne had each attended the School of Agriculture in Lincoln for two terms, which were just for 26 weeks–after fall harvest and before spring planting. I enrolled in fall of 1916. In February I came home with Scarlet Fever. Two weeks after the start of S of A [spring] *term, Mother thought the epidemic had abated so if I avoided crowds I might reenter S of A. When graduating in April 1921 I received also a teachers certificate. I was hired for Rohrs school* [located 3 miles south of Sunny Slope farm] *for the fall. At the County Teachers' Convention we* [i.e. those with only a teacher's certificate] *were advised to attend Peru College summer school. I continued in Peru the following two years* [1922-23 & 1923-24].

[In the fall of 1924 he sent his application to various county school boards.] *One board accepted my application to teach in High School at Malmo, NE. One semester there convinced me I was not adapted to teaching school. I came home to work. In the spring of 1925 I began farming with very limited equipment and no money. I planted corn by listing with a walking lister and 3 horses, then planting with a one-horse drill.*

Aug. 21, 1927, Nainie and I were married. Mother had bought the Rosewood school house, had it moved to the farm, and adapted it for a dwelling.

Pictures of Dad showing him as a member of Nella's family were mentioned previously, but two that portray him individually prior to his marriage appear as Figs. 43 and 44.

Fig. 43 Young Hugh Stoddard   Fig. 44 Hugh Pettet Stoddard

My mother, Nainie L. Robertson, also was born in eastern Nebraska, but she lived in several other places prior to marriage.

Much of Nainie's life as a child was covered well in the diary of her mother (see Chapter 12); but the following two recollections describe some of her fondest ones:

> *Many incidences connected with our train trips come to mind; some are happy, some are sad. It was my job to carry a little sack which held an alcohol stove—a round container of metal about the size of a saucer, with a wick-like top. We took the lid off, poured the alcohol on this wick, then lit it. It made a bluish flame and heated our water for tea on the train. Why the authorities allowed us to have this fire hazard, I cannot tell, but no one questioned or frowned upon it. Thus when Father got off at a town, he dashed into an eating*

place with a little pail to buy coffee. Then he dashed out and got on the train. We kept the coffee hot on our stove. Once in a while he had trouble getting waited on and I sweat fearing that he would get left. I looked out of the windows anxiously until I saw him coming with the pail or the pie, or whatever. Once or twice when he failed to show up before the train began to move, I shed unhappy tears, thinking he had gotten left. But he never did; he always would come walking into the coach after a little bit, carrying our food or coffee.

What joyous hours we spent in the Ford; what scores of short rides we took, mostly on the-spur-of-the-moment affairs. Mother was always ready to go; so at a suggestion from Dad, she and I would hastily change clothing while Dad cranked the flivver. Then away we would go. Our favorite way of entertaining visitors at this time was to take them for a ride after supper. We usually drove out along the scenic Fort Crook Boulevard, down to Avery, and back by the lower road. It was a treat to everybody, jolty and jiggley as the riding was then. Mother was always happiest when out like that with guests; and Dad thrilled to the feel of the wheel.

In 1907 Nainie's parents bought a one-acre place with a six-room house on Fort Crook Boulevard south of South Omaha. She went to fifth grade at Madison School, located almost a mile from her home. She did well in school and she was the top student in her eighth grade class in 1910. She then attended South Omaha High School rather than the nearby school at Bellevue because of the quality of the normal (teacher) training at the former one. In May 1914 she graduated (second in her class) from South High School and was prepared to teach in a rural school. Her plans were to earn enough money from teaching so she could attend the Normal School in Peru.

After failing to obtain an offer to teach in any school in the Omaha area, Nainie wrote to several school boards, each one successively a greater distance from home. She finally accepted a rural school located on the northern edge of Holt County, Nebraska. In September 1914 she left home, took her first train ride, alone, and headed to terra incognita.

Nainie was met at the train station, which was on the north side of the Niobrara River (in Boyd County), by the Noele family. They took her across the river on a rickety "bridge" and thence to their home. She had made arrangements with them for room and board (initially for $3.00 per week, which would approximate $65.00 in today's dollars).

Nainie soon became good friends with the Noele family. Mr. Noele, as president of the school board, kept her school room supplied with teaching items and firewood. Mrs. Noele gave Nainie motherly advice; and Rika, who was a young teenager, was excited about being a friend of this young school teacher.

That first year of teaching in a distant place was a great adventure and made a lasting impression on Nainie. In 1956 she decided to describe her experiences with considerable detail. Her fascinating account of that memorable year radiates her excitement upon experiencing a new cultural environment, with its challenging situations. The following relate to her memories of that year:

> One day Elmer approached me. Are you coming to the dance tonight? I replied, I hadn't heard anything about a dance. "Where is it?" He told me a little about it; then urged me: "Better come." I explained that Noeles did not seem to care for social activities. Then he offered: "Will you go if I get you and Rika?" I said we would.
>
> Rika was quite happy over the prospect; she began speculating as to who Elmer would find to come to get us. "Probably Ed Carlon", she finally said. Ed was an attractive young man – according to what Rika told of him – who lived in an adjoining school district. He helped his Dad farm; he had his own team and buggy.

After supper and dishes, Rika and I slipped upstairs to our room to make ourselves pretty. Rika was unsurprisingly rather excited as this was her first dance. It was my first one, also, and I was also aflutter. I had never attended dances in Omaha for two reasons: my social activities centered around Epworth League meetings and parties, Sunday School, and school parties; my religious training had influenced my belief that dances were wicked and not to be mixed with the church. My hobby was music and I loved rhythm of music and dancing, but I never even thought of going to public dances in Omaha; and our family did not associate with a group who had private dances. When the young folks at Lefler [Methodist Episcopal Church] heard later that fall that Nainie was attending dances, they were a bit shocked perhaps. I felt that the dances held in the homes of the community where I taught were the only means I had of becoming acquainted with the people whom I served. They were mostly like folk dance sessions anyway.

A knock suddenly sounded downstairs; Mrs. Noele opened the kitchen door and Elmer's voice bellowed out: "Are the girls ready?" We went down and out the door. Yes, there was Ed's outfit. Elmer was by the buggy, talking with Ed but we could hear none of it until, "Your woman" came to us in Elmer's voice, followed by his cackle. Elmer had made it very clear to Ed that I was Elmer's partner for that evening.

This small dance was held in a small house, two of the rooms having been stripped of carpets, tables, and all removable furniture. While I sat watching the various couples circling the floor, an attractive young woman came and sat down beside me, introducing herself: "I am Mabel Carlon, Ed's sister." We were attracted to each other from the first minute we met. Between dances that evening we chatted enthusiastically. I met most of the folks there through her friendliness. Since Elmer did not ask for the first dance, I was free to dance with anyone.

Ed asked for a two-step; but I told him I did not know how to dance. Mabel and he urged me on; soon I, too, was on the floor finding it easy indeed to follow Ed's leading. He would not believe, nor would others, that I had never danced before. The square dances were the most fun. I loved the turning, the swinging, the bowing, the carefree happiness of it all. Friendly hands guided if I lost the way. "Big ones swing and little ones, too" sang the caller.

Elmer finally came to claim a two-step. He gripped my two arms with strong hands then holding me thus at arms' length, he swung me round the room in big, free strides. I am sure he felt a bit out of his element for he acted relieved when the music stopped and he could escort me to my seat. (I was glad, too, when the two-step was over.)

When Ed took Rika and me to the next dance (Elmer had said nothing about coming along), he [Ed] *asked me for the first dance and the "Home, Sweet, Home" waltz* [always the special last dance of the evening].

At one dance I met a young, attractive man, Roy Barleson, who lived just out of the district. He was a very modern-looking man, a good dancer and the owner of a fine car. Shortly after I met him, he happened along by the school in his spring wagon; he asked if I were ready to go home, and when I replied in the affirmative he asked me to ride with him. I picked up my raincoat and allowed Roy to help me into the seat. He was very pleasant company; it seemed nice to have such a handsome man interested in me. I had always been so afraid of the boys at grade school – their crude jokes and sometimes obscene language bothered – and I was too timid and afraid to try to interest any boy in

High School. If I admired one I took great care that he did not learn of it. So here in Holt County there were so many men who seemed to like my society and were happy to invite me, that I was thrilled. We reached the Noele home all too soon and Roy helped me down out of the wagon. When I went into the house Mrs. Noele looked at me rather oddly. She proceeded to tell me about Roy Barleson, how he always made over new girls in the community, how he was a lady's man and not always to be trusted.

Ed always came to take me – and quite often, Rika – to the dances. Once Ed and I attended a dance quite a distance away. I remember how bitterly cold it was; and what a tiny house we danced in. Just the kitchen was available; it accommodated just one square of dancers at a time. But everyone made the most of it; everyone had fun. I remember, too, that Ed was specially sweet when we danced the Home-Going Waltz that time.

One Sunday Ed was commissioned by Mabel and her Steady to get me and come over to Carlon's for an evening of games and chatter. He called for me right after dinner. It was a cloudy, threatening day; the wheels squeaked over the cold snow. Suddenly the wind sprang up; some snowflakes swirled around us. I was uneasy at once for I thought that a storm could quickly block the roads and shut me away from my school. That would never do, I pointed out to Ed; I told him I believed we had better turn around and go back. I finally convinced him for there was a feeling of storm in the air. The ride back was more leisurely. From his pocket Ed took a bottle of perfume, a little gift he had bought for me. He took the stopper out and held the bottle toward me, indicating he was going to dump some on me. I shrieked, "Don't." He stopped but not before quite a bit fell on my scarf. We had quite a laugh over the strong scent. The odor hung on that scarf for months, long after I returned home in May. That particular scent held a memory for me for years. The next time I saw Ed after that Sunday he told me what a lot of kidding he had to take because he came home without me. They had been watching for us and had seen us, miles away, pass a certain place. Then they saw the buggy going back the way it had come. "You lost her out of the buggy.", they accused him. "You have to go back and find her." Guess they never did quit kidding him about it – at least as long as I was in the county.

One time Rika, Ed and I went some distance away. The people who had planned the lovely party, had a large house so several Skip-to-Mah-Lou circles could go on at one time. Refreshments were served at a late hour; then everyone left. Benny [an older Noelle son] *was to ride horseback along behind us. Ed usually gave his team their head and they got us home. But this night was different.*

The horses ran right into a snowbank and stopped abruptly. Ed got out; Benny caught up and dismounted. After a bit they came and told me we were off the road, that we'd have to stay there until daylight or the horses were apt to break something floundering around. Benny tied his horse to the back of the buggy; then he climbed in and sat huddling at our feet, with a little of the lap-robe over his knees. We closed our eyes, trying to catnap. I don't believe I slept any; I can't say whether the others did or not. After quite a long time, the dim light of dawn began to steal over the countryside. We stirred; Ed and Benny got out and untied the saddle horse, then backed the team into a safe place. Soon Ed could tell where to guide them; we were on our way again; we came in for a safe landing at seven o'clock when we drove into the Noele yard.

Some years after writing about what she regarded as a very unforgettable year of teaching, Nainie added the following postscript:

> *We* [Ed and I] *wrote to each other the next year; then he came to Burt County to work for his Uncle on the farm. Ed came down to see me and to meet my folks. When he went back he wrote and asked me to marry him. I told him that I was not ready to get married yet; that I was not sure I loved him enough. He said he was not surprised; guess he must have sensed this. One time he got a bit peeved and wrote, "There is just as good fish left in the sea."*

Nainie did not expand on her comments about "not being ready to get married" or "not being sure she loved him enough". This lack of extensive considerations of the pros and cons of marriage to Ed contrasts with her deliberations about marriage to Hugh later (see below). The fact remains that she did not marry Ed and she left that area of Nebraska.

Nainie's activities for the next few years were quite varied. She taught a year in the Nebraska Sandhills (at Josie in 1915-16); attended the Nebraska State Teachers College at Peru (Peru Normal) 1916-17; taught in rural Sarpy County School District #14 near Gretna (where she lived with her brother Dean until he left for war); and taught in a graded rural school in Sarpy County (Sch. Dist. #28) until the outbreak of the influenza pandemic (the 1918 Spanish flu), which was so severe the school was closed for many weeks. She herself got the flu in Feb. 1918, which affected her health so much the following year that she had to resign from her job in another Sarpy County school. She briefly did substitute teaching in the spring of 1920. That summer she left with her parents for the West.

After the family's return to Nebraska in 1921, Nainie went back to Peru Normal to renew her teaching certificate. She then taught at Falls City 1922-23. [N. B. During that year, Della, Dean, and Charlotte – and essentially Nainie – moved to Lincoln.] She finished her teacher training and received her Diploma at Peru Normal in the fall of 1923-24 (Figs. 45 and 46). In 1924-25 she taught briefly at Willard School in Lincoln, but left because of health problems; attended Lincoln Business College, but quit because of continuing poor health.

Fig. 45 Young Nainie Robertson   Fig. 46 Nainie (Robertson) Stoddard

She then began raising chickens at her home (with Della, Dean, and Charlotte) in Lincoln. This was when Nainie wrote in her diary that she was discouraged because of poor health and no marriage prospects.

It was while attending college at Peru that Hugh's sister Lois introduced Nainie and Hugh to each other. I have no record of how the initial relationship developed, but apparently the friendship was close enough that Hugh felt he could write to Nainie during his lonely semester at Malmo High School.

Nainie's response commenced a continuous correspondence almost three years – that is, until the time of their marriage. It is from this voluminous set of letters that one can gain an understanding of her thoughts about, and motives for, her actions.

Unfortunately the letters written by Hugh during this courtship period do not exist because, at some time, Nainie apparently destroyed all of the letters Hugh wrote to her. Nevertheless, some of Hugh's thoughts can be extrapolated by Nainie's comments, as well as from his drafts of two letters (see below).

The first of a enormous collection of letters Nainie wrote to Hugh was sent in October 1924 and the last was in August 1927, a few days before their marriage. Here I have extracted only bits and pieces from her extensive letters. My heavy redaction eliminates her views on a multitude of topics such her judgment about the merits of certain movies, her personal debate about bobbing her hair, her bemusement occasionally with her colleagues, and her lengthy discussions with Hugh about the pros and cons of many decisions. The following letters are ones I believe are the most meaningful:

Oct. 24, 1924, from Box 176 R.4. Lincoln [envelope dated Oct.25 sent to Malmo]

Dear Friend,
Your letter was a nice surprise and I am glad you wrote.
Sunday was a perfect day, and I, too, thought of Peru with her hills and beautiful trees. I generally do in the fall and I always long for one good hike there this time of the year. But there are interesting walks nearer home, but one usually likes company. I haven't forgotten our walk at Peru. Wouldn't it have been fine if the day had been like one of these October days? I appreciated your calls, yours & your sister's, that day. I've often thought of how interested you are in nature.
The district [teachers'] meeting is held here Nov. 5, 6, 7, & 8. If you come to Lincoln call us up. Our number is M3595. We would be glad to have you come to see us; and, if it would be convenient for you to make this your headquarters, we would be glad to have you. We

are within walking distance of the car line. If you come, maybe we can get a walk in – or a ride in our flivver.

I know you will be rather surprised to learn that I am not teaching just now. Ever since High School I have either taught or gone to school, and, as my brother says, I always work too hard at it. When I left Peru last January, I went to raising chickens and, although I worked hard, I felt well and we all thought I needed a little such work, as I've never had a chance to do much else but use my mind.

I had quite a talk with Lefler, the Sup't. here at Lincoln, about my taking a position in his schools. We all thought that, if I found it too much, I could always quit. But I am sorry now that I did not wait another year before trying. Lefler likes my recommendations and he was sorry when I thought the work too heavy. You can't imagine what so much red tape, supervising, & extra meetings mean to the teacher. Lincoln schools are hard at best, but the first year is awful as they have many extra meetings for the new teachers. Omaha, now, is not so particular.

Your friend, Nainie Robertson

Dec.10, 1924, from R.4. Lincoln [envelope dated Dec.12; sent to Malmo]

Dear Mr. Stoddard,

Sorry you did not find us here that Sunday. It was a perfect day for a walk..

Chickens are doing as well as usual these cold days. Hope they keep on.

About your teaching? Well, no matter how many friends or loved ones we can boast, we still live very much alone. We, alone, must really make decisions, meet crises, live, and die. But still, we have the counsel (or is it council) of friends & older people. So you alone must really decide whether you really like teaching. You usually like what you do well, taking everything else into consideration. You have had such a short experience yet that you cannot really judge aright. I believe every teacher at times feels he is a failure and the quicker he gets out of the profession the better.

Personality does play so much in teaching. In my chosen field (Primary) I'm all right, but oh! it does take energy to be a live-wire and make children keep awake and industrious. So much energy that I am beginning to see how hard it is.

Always your friend Nainie Robertson.

June 4, 1925, R.4. Box 176, Lincoln [envelope dated June 5]

Dear Hugh, [N.B. By this date, she used a more familiar greeting.]

As for teaching: Charlotte's friend, Miss Aker, whom you met here, suggested I apply for a rural school near her brother's home. It is a school with only eight pupils in it. I must confess that I had a struggle – what I ought to do vs. what I wish to do. Argument said: "Take it as an easy proposition for a year in which to build up." My mind said, "Think of returning to rural school at this late a day." At first I couldn't think of it. But at last – after a time – I applied. But after being elected, Mr. Leech, my future Sup't. 'phoned me from Lincoln and asked if I would rather have a small Third Grade in town – in Harvard. Only eighteen pupils. Would I? It seemed so much better. So I said yes and have my contract. Somehow I feel at ease now about it.

As always, Nainie Robertson.

Nainie's letters make it evident that she and Hugh visited each other occasionally, but the settings and topics of conversations are unknown. However, I believe that a get-together at her Lincoln home in August (1925) was quite significant because, it appears, the couple broached the possibility of a long-term relationship. This supposition is based partly on the contents of a letter found among Hugh's possessions (after his death). It was addressed to "Dear Chaperon", which means it possibly was a newspaper or magazine column. This draft copy displays much editing and a mixture of several revisions, which leads to uncertainty about the final letter. Nevertheless, the following is probably close to what was mailed to "Dear Chaperon":

> *I am a young man 26 years old. A little more than a year ago I made the acquaintance of a young lady about my own age. I have found we have much in common . . . an interest in me that no other girl ever did. I have found in her the qualities that I hold most important . . . I have been received into her home as a close friend, but circumstances have prevented us going anywhere together or being alone much. I have never felt the thrills of exaltation that I have noticed in the presence of some other girls. I have not felt that indescribable something that makes it seem a little bit of heaven just to be in her presence. In short I have not fallen in love. Does this mean that we were not meant for each other and our hearts will never beat as one or is this attractiveness, this personal magnetism and blessing, which is not bestowed upon all girls or which some do not bring into play? My puzzle is this: having found that I am not attracted to this girl must I conclude that we would not be happy together?*
>
> *Uncertain*

In the fall of 1925 Nainie began teaching at Harvard, Nebraska, from where she wrote a flurry of letters to Hugh. She referred occasionally to various times they met, but the details of their times together were often skimpy. However, the writings by Nainie and Hugh refer to a momentous event, one that occurred at Christmas time at Sunny Slope Farm. That meeting was verified partly by an entry Lois made in her diary on Dec. 26, 1925: "Some time ago we invited Hugh's lady friend, Miss Nainie Robertson, of Lincoln, to spend part of her vacation with us. She came on Tuesday P.M. and left on Thursday P.M. We enjoyed her visit very much, and think that she is very much of a lady." Also, Nainie wrote in her skimpy diary: "I am engaged to Hugh Pettet Stoddard of Auburn, Nebr. – became engaged at Xmas time of '25."

Among Hugh's stored papers is a rough draft of a letter written by him shortly after Christmas of 1925. The version that remains has many phrases crossed out and others inserted so the final wording of what was sent is unknown. It appears he wanted her to think very seriously about the consequences of deciding to abandon her current job, which she enjoyed so much, and her city home with its many amenities. Furthermore, he warned her about the consequences of becoming a farm wife in a rural community, one that tended to be closed to outsiders. His message follows:

> *Dear Nainie:*
>
> *I have mailed three letters since I saw you this week but I can not say how many messages I have composed but left unwritten. Shortly after you returned home two dark pictures kept appearing before me. I wanted to tell you but I knew I should not turn your attention from your work just when you were returning to it, and besides why should I reiterate a bad dream. Yet I felt that the letters I did write showed a little reserve so I tell you now what was troubling me.*
>
> *Though I had seen it time and again before – I could ignore it no longer. The expanse – the contrast between us – between your life as it has been and what it might be on a farm. It seemed it would be stripped of so much, so narrowed, so then I prayed over and over that I might be worthy of the one I loved. But you saw so little opportunity to accomplish what you might in the world.*
>
> *I wondered if I could ever give another a place in my thoughts. Oh, the picture grows darker for the one I love has disregarded self to make life happy for me.*

Why did she do it! Though she tries to hide it, I see now and then a longing look. Day after day the same routine. Seldom even a neighbor stops on an errand. The people here have not the culture or refinement to make their friendship what one wishes for. Opportunities for good entertainment are few. Even the church seems cold and lifeless. My people are not what her people are. I am not what she is. Nothing could make me more unhappy than to know I had made a loved one unhappy.

Perhaps it was the folks' sickness that brought on such an attack of the blues for the next day I recognized only the dim outline of these pictures but I saw where they had been. A very plain little house with improvised furniture but the nucleus of a home, where we shall be happy because we have each other.

We will begin painting a beautiful picture . . . In school all students meet as equals, but how little each knows of the others outside of school. As a successful teacher and a fellow Christian, you offered a helping hand. To one in trouble, you gave equally comfort and cheer. To one in despair, you gave new hope. To a lonesome soul, you have been a dear friend.

There are so many pleasures and comforts that it would be impossible for us to have–that have always been a part of your life. Oh you would take no thought of this, for your self is one of giving and not receiving. But your chance to give of your God-given talents might be so narrowed that in your heart you would feel that you were not living up to your possibilities. You foresaw this and, I wondered . . . But I prayed that I might be worthy of the one I loved.

I hesitate now to show you these ghost pictures yet they may help to explain why I approached the subject from the angle I did. One other thing completes my explanation. We can never do for our mothers what they have done for us, but I have promised myself never again to go so far from Mother that I can not see her at least once each week.

Nainie, I have tried to put aside my longing while I wrote this one letter. I hope it does not seem too cold, for you are not only the guiding star but the sunshine of my life. Now if you will help me, we will burn these pictures so that they may never be seen again and . . .
[N .B. The writing appears to end here.]   *Hugh*

Admittedly many engaged couples have doubts about upcoming marriages so Hugh's misgivings are not too surprising. In contrast, the letters Nainie sent soon after Hugh wrote his concerns do not seem to share any reservations about going ahead with marriage. Apparently she was ready to become Hugh's wife because her apprehension soon focused more on matters of when to publicly announce their engagement and how such a revelation would affect her job and her relations with her friends. Later her thoughts turned to their future place of residence, and a specific date for their wedding. Some of these worries are manifested in the following letters:

Saturday, [probably Mar. 13, 1926] *Harvard, Nebr*

Dear Hugh,

It seems that I must think it over a bit more. If you think it best that I sign my contract (when it comes) I will surely do it. And we will be patient, too.

About the home, wait a little, please. Your mother must not be hurried or pushed, and let us not be in a hurry to say one way or the other, and so don't speak of it to outsiders.

I would like to ask if the addition [to the school building/house] *would be so large as the part now standing. It looks smaller in the plan. I don't know about the part of living so close* [to your mother].

Wouldn't it be heavenly, Hugh, if we didn't have to wait and to wonder what we should do. Just imagine being able to step into a little home – soon – and being happy!

I am yours, Nainie.

Sunday 10:30 A.M. [probably June 7, 1926, after having been at Sunny Slope]

Your mother said to me, I understand that you & Hugh have decided to walk down life's pathway together–have you? And I said yes and she went on to say how sorry she is that finances are keeping us apart, another year and all. She is very sincere about it, and her saying that meant quite a little bit to me because she hasn't said anything like that to me. But I hadn't said anything to either her or Lois. But my desire is to be all I should be to you & to my in-laws.

Please be so very nice to your mother now as it means a tug to lose her boy, if one may say lose. I know you are good to her and to everyone, so the expression of that command (?) was more to show you how I feel, and how much I appreciate your goodness to her. You need not be told.

Yours. (Lonesome – that's all).

June 18, 1926
Dear Hugh,

Of course Dean & Charlotte now know what I suspect they suspected – that you and I are engaged. I had not told them before. I do not expect to announce my engagement at Harvard until next spring, for many reasons.

Yes, I know you love me. But it seems that a woman knows and yet doesn't know a man loves her. She's a paradox by nature. She wants the one to tell her so even if she knows it. Love to a man is a thing apart–but it's women's whole existence.

Do you know the date of the day we met first?
Yours

Oct. 5, 1926, Harvard

Dear Hugh,
Will it be too late for me to go by train to see you on Sat., Nov. 6th? Let me know.
My! I hope that nice-looking building may be moved cheaply, don't you? I like it very much. Won't it be fun planning things?
I know I shall like it down there. My heart goes pit-a-pat just to think of all this.
Hoping all will work out well, I will sign my name as your loving pal.

Numerous comments in Nainie's letters indicated how much the promise of her own home meant to her. The building that was to be modified into a residence was one of the school buildings the Brock School District sold when a new consolidated schoolhouse was constructed. The following entry from the 1926 diary of Lois (Hugh's sister) explains Nella's decision to provide a home for Hugh and his bride:

I want to write about a new venture in our family. After much grave and thotful consideration, Mother decided to buy a house (provided it would not cost too much) and move it here for Hugh and his fiancée, after their marriage. He wants to farm the place, and we want to have him, and even if he could rent a [different] nearby farmhouse, that would be quite inconvenient, and moreover he wants to make a [permanent] home. So after some inquiries, Mother went to Brock, the day the rural schoolhouses were sold at public auction and she purchased Rosewood [School] for $100.

Nainie was down for less than 24 hours at the time of the State Teacher's Association Meetings [which meant she had a few days with no teaching obligations]. *She is much pleased with the location* [which was located a few hundred yards from the house in which Nella and Lois lived].

After Nainie made that quick trip to Sunny Slope Farm to see the building that would become her future home, she returned to Lincoln where she stayed the few days of the Nebraska Teachers' Convention. After going back to Harvard to resume her teaching, she continued her letters as follows:

Nov. 7, 1926, Harvard

Dear Hugh,

My trip up on the train was an easy, quiet one, full of sweet memories of you standing by the Ford – the glimpse I had just as the train pulled out. So I dreamed of one who is so kind and thoughtful and good – too good to me. I wonder then that I get shy and the shyness makes me dumb when I would speak to express my appreciation of some gift or act of thoughtfulness for me. As a result of this I often speak lightly of something which touches me – maybe others don't understand. But you do – that's the beauty of you & your friendship, which means all the world to me.

Now I have so much to think about, and it is easier to plan since I've seen things for myself. I'll try to write just how I think and then you do as you think best. It would be fine if you owned it [the house] *so I could put some money into it also. But I surely appreciate being so near your work. Such a fine building, and such good neighbors.*

Yours with happy thoughts, & lovely anticipation as regards my gift.

Nainie

Mar. 24, 1927, Harvard

Dear Hugh,

Mother speaks of you as tho' you already were her son-in-law. She has perfect confidence in you and I'm so glad she feels that way. But mother is sort of bitter of late years about so many things. It hurts me so, and I get so upset when I go home, I feel relieved when back here, sometimes. I said to her [when she implied that a mere farmer was not worthy of her daughter], *"You mustn't discourage Hugh about farming."*

Is ever a mother satisfied? I doubt if your mother is – for her boy. But I'm not worried! I know my mother knows I'm in good hands when I marry you – and I know so also. She likes you, Hugh, dear.

Oh Hugh! I hope the sun shines again in your heart. Mine hasn't dimmed for I feel it's all right. And may God help you to see it right too.

From one who loves you most.

Mar. 27, Harvard

Dear Hugh,

I think our courtship is a little odd in two ways. The age-old way is: a young man calls on his lady-love about twice a week. He sees her regularly, about two or three hours only at a time. One evening might be spent on the front porch, the other at some entertainment. There is rarely an entertainment at our church on Sat. and you have never suggested a show or a drive. So it has been hard, especially when roads and weather prevent a drive or a walk when we might be alone. We used to sit in the swing, but when it's been so cold and disagreeable we couldn't. As far as shows and such are concerned, one can't talk in them. I'd love to have it so we could get out and walk, as we usually did. Of course Dean's entertainment kept the folks up and so we couldn't stay up after they left for a heart-to-heart talk. Both evenings were so spent [which did not allow much time for privacy]. *Well, it's all right any way, isn't it, when there is enough faith to bridge the gap. Aren't you absolutely sure of me? Do you doubt?*

Always

Apr. 1, 1927, Harvard Friday

Dear Hugh,

It is always your prerogative to take the initiative. I said that I am shy in your presence, hiding my emotions. Our family always has. So perhaps it makes me sedate. I don't feel prim a bit. (So perhaps, Hugh, it's your own fault you were disappointed. Women love men who demand – when their demands are not selfish.). I wonder if that is true. When I said your own fault my eyes held a twinkle, and I felt mischievous. I've been accused of being a person who likes to tease.

My love to Lois & Mrs. Stoddard and to You.

In early June (1927), Nainie made a trip to Sunny Slope farm. During her visit, she joined the immediate family and the Dougherty clan for a picnic under large walnut trees in the southwest corner of the farm.

By this time the courtship phase had evolved into a discussion about the nitty-gritty of matrimonial planning. With the self-constraints of wooing finished, they began expressing their individual perspectives about several details. For example, Nainie thought a trip to Ni agara Falls would be splendid, but Hugh suggested a family picnic. They also had some trouble deciding on a firm date for their marriage. The following letters from Nainie reflect these issues:

June 8 from Lincoln

Dear Hugh,

I will soon set the date so as to have a few announcement cards printed. I'll surely tell you & ask you first, too.

Yours till Niagara Falls, Nan.

June 17, 1927 Lincoln, Nebr.

Dear Hugh,

Polishing and refining – I think marriage is good for one and all, because it is a sort of discipline – to learn to live so near another, yet to be fair, unselfish, and willing to give the other liberty. We must not insist on our own way too much, nor intrude on the other's own personal affairs. Common property and interests only are ours.

I am perfectly satisfied now: our differences are all over and we understand each other. Believe me when I say I'm anxious to be at work down there–now that proves how much better I'm feeling–and it is worth it. So be patient – entirely so – won't you & know I'll say now when it's best [for the wedding date].

Yours – Nainie

Aug. 3 Wednesday from Lincoln

Dear Hugh,

As to Sunday: if we are married Aug.14 I don't believe we'd want to go on the picnic, however lovely it would be. If we are married on Aug.21 you could suit yourself about going on the picnic Aug.14, but it seems to me we have much to look forward to and would not feel the need. Of course the folks count the few days left, and perhaps the one or two Sundays between now & then, would be appreciated by them.

Afterwards, it will be easy to go on a picnic and much less driving and so less expense as well as energy. I know you feel like you'd like to celebrate after being thru threshing.
    Nan.

Aug. 10, Wednesday, from Lincoln

Dear Hugh,
    It has been in my mind for a long time what our plans had been for today. Now, it seems to me you and I had better go ahead and get married on the twenty-first, regardless of anything else. Shall we?

They did, indeed, marry on Sunday, the 21ˢᵗ of August (Fig. 47). With that act, Nainie forsook the conveniences of city life to live in a house with no electricity or indoor plumbing.

Fig. 47. Hugh and Nainie Wedding Day"

She immediately returned to raising chickens and accepted the customary duties of a farm wife (Fig. 48). During the Depression and drought years of the early to mid 1930s, Nainie and Hugh endured the hardship of a meager income.

Fig. 48. Nainie and Hugh Stoddard, 1931

As the couple grew closer in their affection for each other, Nainie became enamored with life on the farm. Her genuine fondness of living in a rural environment was much deeper than merely the conveniences of electricity and indoor plumbing (which were installed several years later). Soon she truly loved being in tune with Nature – the feelings that were already deep-seated in Hugh's psyche. And, with the arrival of three children, Nainie and Hugh experienced the satisfaction of a closely knit family.

A fitting memorial to what attracted this couple to a place called Sunny Slope Farm is the poem that Nainie wrote in 1956:

Hills of Home

I like the sun-kissed, rock-strewn slopes
Across the creek, up on the hill.
I pick my path; and also stones,
The brightest ones, my pockets fill.

I sit me down on smooth rock ridge,
I sun myself and gaze around.
Our buildings, stock and neighbor's homes,
And distant landscapes – all are found.

I like the lonesome stony spot
I like to sit and look and laze.
Unmindful moments, these are mine
To sooth the pricks of hectic days.

How lucky is my fate, to have
Such space, such chance to roam
Across the fields, the creek, the farm.
Our cherished 'hills of Home'.